OF TIME AND SPACE,

OF GOD AND MAN

by

Hilarion M. Henares Jr.
of the Philippines
2018

Published by **Tatay Jobo Elizes**, Self-Publisher

This book is published and printed under the expressed permission of the author, **HILARION (LARRY) HENARES Jr.**, compiled for this purpose of making his books and all his writings available to the public and promote reading among Filipinos, young and old. The author owns the copyrights to his writings. Author can ask to withdraw his permission to publish his book anytime. Printing of this book is using the present day method of Print-On-Demand (POD) system, where prints will never run out of copies. Author is free to republish or reprint with other publishers and printers anytime.

KDP ISBN Code

ISBN – 9781791954550

Disclaimer: Views are expressed by the author alone. Tatay Jobo Elizes does not knowingly publish false information and may not be held liable for the views of the author exercising his right to free expression.

Self-Publisher's Details:
Contact: job_elizes@yahoo.com
Websites: http:tinyurl.com/mj76ccq +
www. tatayjoboelizes.webs.com +
www.philippinefolio.com

PREFACE

OF TIME AND SPACE, OF GOD AND MAN

At the age of 94, so close to the time of the Grim Reaper, when I shall finally meet my Maker, I choose to embark on a Search for Truth, relying on what I learned as a Catholic (which I still am) at the feet of my Jesuit teachers; on the 25,500 books I read (a book a day from the age of 10 to 70); on two books by Yuval Noah Harari, called to my attention by a fervent Christian Fundamentalist who regards them as bovine ordure; and a book by Steven Pinker from the father of my Swiss daughter-in-law. This journey brought me through unexpected byways from the Big Bang, Time and Timeless Space, the inspiring concept of God and the entire evolution and progress of the Human Race, to the Final Destiny of Man.

TABLE OF CONTENTS

Chapter 1.
Sapiens, a brief history of mankind

Yuval Noah Harari has a perfect prologue to his book, *Sapiens*:

About 13.5 billion years ago, matter, energy, time and space came into being in what is known as the Big Bang. The story of these fundamental features of our universe is called **physics**.

About 300,000 years after their appearance, matter and energy started to coalesce into complex structures, called atoms, which then combined into molecules. The story of atoms, molecules and their interactions is called **chemistry**.

About 3.8 billion years ago, on a planet called Earth, certain molecules combined to form particularly large and intricate structures called organisms. The story of organisms is called **biology**.

About 70,000 years ago, organisms belonging to the species Homo Sapiens started to form even more elaborate structures called **cultures.** The subsequent development of these human cultures is called **history**.

Three important revolutions shaped the course of history: the **Cognitive Revolution** kick-started history about 70,000 years ago; the **Agricultural Revolution** sped it up about 12,000 years ago; and the **Scientific Revolution** which started only 500 years ago, may well end history and start something completely different.

The book, Sapiens, tells the story of how these three revolutions have affected humans and their fellow organisms. Only 6 million years ago, a single female ape had two daughters: one became the ancestor of all chimpanzees; the other became the ancestor of the human race. Just as the cat family had the lions, tigers, cougars, cheetas and the household cats as separate species and cousins, the genus Homo (which we will call Humans) consisted of at least seven species: Sapiens, Neanderthal, Erectus, Soloensis, Floresienses, Donisova.

Of these seven, Homo Erectus is the most durable of all, existing for 2 million years and became extinct 73,000 years before Homo Sapiens even existed. Erectus endured more than Sapiens, which existed for only 70,000 years, and in less than a 1,000 years hence will probably evolve by restructuring its own DNA, to a higher type of Humans.

For a long long time, the Human was an animal of no consequence, not on top of the food chain, but solidly in the middle, confined to hunting small animals like rabbits and avoiding being eaten by larger predators like lions. Humans have a bigger brain than other animals, but had little to show for it but flint knives and pointed sticks. It was only 400,000 years ago that humans began to hunt large game on a regular basis, and only in the last 100,000 years – with the rise of Homo Sapiens – that humans jumped to the top of the food chain.

Other animals on top of that pyramid, like lions, evolved so slowly that nature was able to evolve checks and balances that prevented them from wreaking too much havoc: as lions became deadlier, gazelles evolved to run faster, hyenas to cooperate better, and rhinos to be nastier and more bad-tempered.

With the taming of fire, humans made a spectacular leap to the top of the heap, leaving the whole world totally unprepared for the consequences. When humans domesticated fire, they gained control over an obedient and potentially limitless force. They now have a dependable source of light and warmth, and a deadly weapon against prowling lions. But the best thing about fire is that it allowed humans to cook. Foods that humans cannot digest in their natural forms, such as wheat, rice and potatoes, became staples of the human diet because of cooking, which also changed its chemistry and biology as well. Cooking killed germs and parasites that infested food. Humans also had an easier time chewing and digesting old favorites such as fruits, nuts, insects and carrion if they were cooked. While chimpanzees spend five hours a day chewing raw food, a single hour sufficed for humans eating cooked food. The domestication of fire was a sign of things to come.

Yet despite the benefits of fire, 150,000 years ago, humans were still marginal creatures, no more than a million beings between the Indonesian archipelago and the Spanish peninsula, hardly a blip on the ecological calendar, our own Sapiens with only 10,000 in population, minding its own business in a small corner of eastern Africa.

Those who watched Carl Sagan's original TV series 34 years ago, will remember the cosmic calendar, which is a way to conceptualize the age of the universe (13.8 billion years). If the age of the universe were compressed into one year… in the first second, 12:00:01 AM on January 1 of the Cosmic Year, the Big Bang, the universe was born from a single atom… in the last tick of last second, 12:00 PM of December 31 of the Cosmic Year, man landed on the moon. In-between is the entire history of the Universe. On January 14, appeared Light in the form of a gamma ray burst; on January 22, the first small galaxy appeared; on March 15 our galaxy, the Milky Way, was born of stardust; on September 2, the Solar System was formed; on September 6, our own earth was born 4.5 billion years ago, followed by the moon; on September 14, 3.5 billion years ago, life originated under the oceans, made out of single-celled creatures, eating each other; on November 9, one single cell could not ingest the other single cell it had just eaten, and the multi-celled creature came into being on December 5; and on December 7, sex was born and saw an explosion of life on earth, finally dominated by the dinosaurs; on December 20, the first plant and flower appeared; on December 30, an asteroid was deflected in its path and collided with the earth, killing all the dinosaurs, 13.5 million years ago; the earth tilted 23 degrees from its axis, and the seasons were born in the northern and southern hemispheres; 14 minutes before midnight on the last day of the Cosmic Year, Humans evolved, as hunters and gatherers and that started the Cognitive Revolution that catapulted him to the top of the food chain; two minutes later, 12 minutes to midnight, Man painted his first picture; one minute and 32 seconds, 10,000 years ago, agriculture was invented, starting the Agricultural Revolution; the next second was the end of the Ice Age; at 12 seconds to midnight, the Egyptian and Chinese Civilization came into being; 11 seconds to midnight the first writing appeared and the wheel was invented; 6 seconds to midnight, Buddha, Confucius, Euclid and Archimedes were born; 5 seconds before midnight Jesus and the Roman Empire were born, and the number zero was invented; 4 seconds to midnight Mohammad, the Maya Civilization and the Byzantine Empire came into being; 2 seconds to midnight, the Mongol Empire, the Crusades, Christopher Columbus, the Renaissance and Johann Sebastian Bach, Shakespeare happened; and 1 second to midnight, Isaac Newton and the Scientific Revolution came into being; in the last second of the cosmic year, the World War I, World War II, Albert Einstein, Karl Marx, Adolf Hitler, and President Franklin Delano Roosevelt came into being. And on the last tick of the last second, man landed on the moon.

The Cognitive Revolution began 70,000 years ago, and lasted for 58,000 years, the longest and the most significant event in the history of the humans, it saw domestication of fire, the death of over a thousand species of plant and animals, the demise of all other Human species, and the rise of Sapiens as the deadliest serial killer of all time, and the sole master of the planet Earth.

The Agricultural Revolution started 12,000 years ago and lasted 11,500 years; the hunt-and-gather ecosystem which can only support about 10 million inhabitants, ended with domestication of plants and animals, which brought about an ecosystem that could support 7 billion inhabitants, most of them on the verge of starvation. And we saw the birth of Great Civilizations: the greatness that was Egypt, the Wonder that was China, the Grandeur that was Rome, and the Glory that was Greece; and the rise of modern religions based on alpha-male Fatherhood (Judaism, and its derivatives, Christianity and Islam), as well as rational religions by Great Teachers Confucius and Buddha.

The Scientific Revolution was born only 500 years ago, along with the Enlightenment, Age of Discovery, Capitalism, Industrialization, and the three of the most staggering developments of all: (1) exploiting the power of suns and stars, (2) reaching out to the timeless space beyond our planet, (3) probing the secrets of the DNA, and controlling our own evolution.

The next essay is about the Cognitive Revolution, the rise of Sapiens as lord and master.

Chapter 2.
The Cognitive Revolution

Having a skeleton which evolved for millions of years to walk on four legs, with a relatively smaller head, Humans walking upright, suffered from back-aches and stiff necks. The female of the species fared worse, because an upright gait required narrower hips, constricting the birth canal (at the time human brains grew larger), forcing her to give birth prematurely when the baby was still small. This means the Humans at birth are still underdeveloped. A colt can trot at birth, but a human baby is helpless when born, dependent for many years on their elders for sustenance, protection and education. Mothers of early humans could hardly forage for food with needy children in tow, and required constant help from family members, friends and neighbors to raise her child. It took a tribe to raise a child. Evolution favored those with strong social ties. And since humans are born underdeveloped, they could be educated and socialized to a far greater extent than other animals. A larger brain had little to show for its use, but flint knives and pointed sticks.

Even from the very beginning, the Genus Homo, whom we refer to as Humans, of which there were at least six species other than Sapiens (Neanderthals, Erectus, Soloensis, Floresiensis, Rudolfensis, Denisova) had notably large brains that require 25% of the human's energy when the body is at rest, compared to only 8% of other apes' energy when at rest. We humans are so enamored of our high intelligence, that we assume the more the brain power the better. This is not true for the early humans, whose energy is needed more for the physical exertion of foraging for food and running away from large predators. What really jumpstarted the development of the Humans far ahead of the rest of animals are (1) the domestication of fire as a source of light, warmth, and protection against predators, but more important for cooking foods that are indigestible in their natural state, like wheat, rice and potatoes, and (2) most important of all, the development of a unique language that lent itself to gossiping, and telling stories about things that do not exist – the appearance of a new way of thinking and communicating, between 70,000 and 30,000 years ago, that constitutes the Cognitive Revolution.

Social cooperation is our key to survival and reproduction. It is not enough for individual men and women to know the whereabouts of predators like lions and preys like deer. It is more important for them to know who in their tribe hates whom, who is sleeping with whom, who is honest, who is a cheat – reliable information about who could be trusted, meant that small bands could expand into larger bands, that humans could develop tighter and more sophisticated types of cooperation. But the most unique part of the language of the Homo Sapiens is its ability to transmit information about things that do not exist at all, about entities that they have never seen, touched or smelled. Legends, myths, gods and religions appeared for the first time during the Cognitive Revolution. Telling stories of fiction allowed us not merely to imagining things, but also to do it and **believe it collectively**. We can weave common myths like the biblical creation story, nationalist myths of modern states like (hahaha) American Exceptionalism, and legal fiction of the existence of corporations, money and financial instruments – such myths allow Sapiens to cooperate flexibly in large numbers. Ants and bees cooperate too in large numbers, but they do so rigidly and only with close relatives. Wolves and chimpanzees do so far more flexibly than ants, but they do so only with small numbers of individuals that they know intimately. Sapiens can cooperate in extremely flexible ways with countless numbers of strangers. That is why we Sapiens rule the world, while ants eat our leftovers, and chimps are locked up in zoos and research laboratories.

Whenever Sapiens arrives at a new location, the local population become extinct. The last remains of Homo Soloensis dated 50,000 years ago, of Denisova shortly thereafter, Neanderthals about 30,000 years ago, the dwarf-like Floresiensis about 12,000 years ago. Mostly domesticated, animals now serve as meat and galley slaves in Sapiens' Noah's Ark.

Chapter 3.
The Agricultural Revolution

For 2.5 million years, humans fed themselves by gathering plants and hunting animals that lived and bred in the wild, without their intervention. All this changed about 10,000 years ago, when Homo Sapiens, the last and lone survivor of the 7 human species, began to devote almost all of their time and effort to domesticating a few plant and animal species -- which they thought would provide them with more fruit, grain and meat – a revolution in the way humans lived – the Agricultural Revolution.

Scholars once proclaimed this a great leap forward for humanity, for indeed this led to the production of food so prodigious that it resulted in an exponential increase of population and the rise of great civilizations, among them the Greatness that was Egypt, the Wonder that was China, the Grandeur that was Rome, the Glory that was Greece; also the rise of great religions, Judaism and its derivatives, Christianity and Islam; as well as cultures inspired by two great teachers, Buddha and Confucius.

Yet Yuval Noah Harari calls the Agricultural Revolution the greatest fraud in all history, an irreversible disaster that left the ordinary human beings infinitely worse than ever before, a disaster perpetrated not by kings or priests, but by a handful of lowly plant species: wheat, rice, corn which, in the past, have been nothing but wild grasses of little significance:

1.	These few plants manipulated and domesticated Homo Sapiens rather than vice-versa. Think about it. As hunters and gatherers, Sapiens lived a comfortable life, spending time in more stimulating and varied ways; as farmers, they were forced to work from dawn to dusk taking care of their wheat and rice fields, which demanded much from them. These grasses did not like rocks, trees and other plants, so farmers broke their backs clearing, furrowing and weeding the fields under the scorching sun; these grasses were always thirsty for water, so farmers dug irrigation canals and carried heavy buckets of water from wells; these grasses are attacked by rabbits and locusts, so farmers built fences and stood guard; these grasses were subject to worms and blight and needed nourishment, so farmers provided composts and animal feces to fertilize the fields. For this miserable life of hard labor from dawn to dusk, what did Sapiens get in return?

2.	For one thing, the human body evolved in the past 2.5 million years, for climbing trees, for running after rabbits and running from lions, and not for digging ditches, clearing rocks and carrying buckets of water. Human spines, knees, necks and arches paid the price. Ancient skeletons show that the transition to agriculture brought about ailments seldom experienced by hunter-gatherers: slipped discs, arthritis, hernias, fallen arches, dislocated bones, etcetera.

3.	Agriculture offered more food, but not a better diet. Remember we are omnivorous apes who thrive on a wide variety of foods. Grains like wheat, rice and corn made up only very small fraction of the diet of the hunter-gatherer. A diet based on cereals is poor in minerals and vitamins, hard to digest, and really bad for our teeth and gums, so that we are all overfed and undernourished.

4.	Agriculture did not bring economic security. Hunter-gatherers relied on dozens of animal species of plants and animals to survive, and rarely died of starvation or disease; if deer and wild potatoes are unavailable, they could always switch to hunting rabbits and eat wild strawberries. Farmers, until only very recently, relied for a great bulk of their calorie intake, on a small variety of domesticated plants, often on a single staple like rice, wheat or corn. If the rains failed or clouds of locusts come, or if a fungus infected the fields, peasants die by the thousands and millions.

5.	Because Agriculture tied the farmers to the land, the farming community settled in towns near the fields they tilled, and that changed their way of life for the worse forever. Forced to live together in large numbers, Sapiens not only died of starvation and violence, but also of infectious diseases. For all the time during the 10,000 years of the Agricultural Revolution, mankind was cursed by the Four Horsemen of the Apocalypse: Famine, Pestilence, War and Death.

Hunters and foragers are relatively less subject to violence from fellow humans than farmers are. For one thing, hunters with knives, spears and arrows, can fight back. For another, hunters have no fixed address and have no possessions worth robbing. But farmers have a houseful of furniture, clothes and personal possessions, a barn full of stored hay and grain, carefully tended animals, and fields of carefully cultivated plants, all worth defending, but having converted their weapons to plowshares, farmers have very little ability to defend themselves from human predators. It is this situation that lead to Feudalism, the divine right of kings, a pampered idle elite of priests and learned men, and whole civilizations!

Bands of brigands, probably former hunters, preyed on farmers, who are the only source of wealth in an agricultural society, mostly killing them for their possessions. A smart farmer says to the brigand: "This is all counter-productive. If you kill us all, there will be no one to farm the lands. There is plenty of food to go around, so why don't we just give you part of the wealth we make, and you promise to protect us from other brigands." And this is how the protection racket which American gangsters employ so efficiently, came into being. The brigands were convinced that this was an excellent arrangement, and to protect each other, all brigands agreed not to fight each other, but to divide the entire area into exclusive monopolies among bands of brigands.

Over time, after collecting tributes from the farmers, they imagined that they really owned the lands, and the tributes extorted were taxes paid by the farmers to self-styled nobles who govern them. To further stabilized the Feudal System, they chose the meanest, sexiest and strongest brigand of all, to be their king, and mobilized a church to give this piece of shit the Divine Right of Kings straight from God. From this pampered and idle elite of priests and nobles emerged learned men who organized cities, laws and courts, armies and nations, and civilizations that built roads, bridges, the pyramids, the Great Wall of China; invented numerals and the concept of zero.

The evolution of Religion during the Agricultural Revolution is worrisome. *"There in the beginning was Isis, oldest of the old; she was the first goddess from whom all becoming arose."* All religions in the ancient civilizations were originally founded on the Female Principle, based on the concept of Mother-Creator, who was a tolerant God, devoid of self-righteous bigotry and obsessive aversion to sex, democratic in her acceptance of all other gods into her pantheon. The emergence of Judaism and its derivatives, Christianity and Islam, based on the Male Principle and the Father-Creator who was intolerant of all other gods, *"I am the Lord thy God. Thou shalt not have strange gods before me!"* was profoundly unsettling on human civilization, leading us directly into the Dark Ages of the first millennium. Jews and Christians were politely invited by Romans to enroll their God into the pantheon where a family of gods adopted from the Greeks were already enrolled. Shouting, "There is no God but Jehovah, and all of you heathens will go to hell!" Jews and Christians were considered by the Romans, subversive of public order, and had to be expelled and persecuted, in a manner they thoroughly deserved. The Jews were an exclusive entity united only by blood, and were easily expelled and dispersed. The Christians were different, under St. Paul, they welcomed Gentiles as well, especially Roman citizens. Under the regime of Emperor Constantine, Christians outnumbered all others in the Roman Empire, and Constantine declared himself Emperor of the Holy Roman Empire, with the Holy Roman Catholic Church as the official religion. The Catholic Church perpetuated itself by a document called *Constitutum Constantini,* the Donation of Constantine, which gave the Church spiritual and political dominion over the entire world, which was ultimately proven a fake and a fraud in the 18th century. After being valid for 70% of the Church's existence, its effects proved irreversible. Jesuits declared the fraud a "historical necessity," engineered by God, – in pursuit of the end that justifies the means.

Less worrisome is the evolution of Law and Social Order under the Agricultural Revolution. The settlement of Sapiens in villages, cities, nations and empires, necessitated the emergence of central government based on the cooperation of thousands, even millions of human beings. Such cooperation can be achieved, as we explained before, by the creation of myths that all believe in, and that included laws that guarantee justice for all. Of all that humans aspire to, love has to be earned, mercy begged for, but justice was something that is demanded by all citizens. The first legal system was promulgated by King Hammurabi of Mesopotamia in 1776 BC, and this gradually evolved 3,552 years later, by coincidence in 1776 AD, to that drafted by Thomas Jefferson as the American Declaration of Independence. Both documents invoked the authority of God – the Babylonian deities, Anu, Enlil and Marduk, by the Code of Hammurabi; the Christian "Creator", by the preamble of the Declaration of Jefferson. Both proclaimed God-given principles, "the course of truth and the correct way of life" by Hammurabi, and "certain unalienable rights" that are "self-evident" by Jefferson. Both documents are fictional myths created in the minds of those who drafted and those who believed in them.

The Code of Hammurabi rooted in universal and eternal principles of justice dictated by the gods, promulgated a system of hierarchy in which people are divided into 2 genders, male and female, and three classes, superior people, commoners and slaves. The preamble of the Declaration is much more majestic and believable today: *We hold these truths to be self-evident, that all men are created equal, that they are endowed by their Creator with certain unalienable rights, that among these are life, liberty and the pursuit of happiness;* believable indeed until the Age of Reason and Science, when biology proves that people are not "created equal" but evolved instead not to be equal, for Evolution is based on difference in genetic code and environmental influences, not equality; and that there is no Creator, only a blind evolutionary process, devoid of any purpose, leading to the birth of individuals. "Created equal" should be translated into "evolved differently"; and "endowed by their Creator" should be translated simply into "born."

Also, there are no such things as "unalienable rights" in biology, only only organs, abilities and characteristics that are not unalienable, but subject to constant mutations and may well be completely lost over time. Birds fly, not because they have a right to fly, but because they have wings; the ostrich is one bird that over time, lost its ability to fly; therefore, "unalienable rights" should be translated into "mutable characteristics." And what are the characteristics that evolved in humans? Life, certainly; but Liberty? There is no such thing in Biology. Like Equality, Human Rights and corporate rights, Liberty is something that people invented and exists only in their imagination. From a biological viewpoint, it is meaningless to say that citizens in a democracy are free while citizens in a dictatorship are unfree. And how about happiness? So far, Biology has found no way to define happiness, or a way to measure it objectively; Biology acknowledges the existence of pleasure which is more easily defined and measured. So "life, liberty and the pursuit of happiness" should be translated into "life and the pursuit of pleasure."

So here is that line in Jefferson's Declaration, translated from fiction to fact in scientific biological terms: *We hold these truths to be self-evident, that all men evolved differently, that they are born with certain mutable characteristics, and among these are life and the pursuit of pleasure.*

Advocates of equality and human rights, as well as of American Exceptionalism (hahaha) may be outraged by this line of reasoning, but so what? Such fictional myths are not evil conspiracies or useless mirages. They are the only useful way large numbers of humans can operate effectively and forge a better society -- valid at the time of King Hammurabi 3,552 years ago, valid today at the time of Donald Trump and the white trash that elected him to office.

The creation of myths that all believe in, including laws guarantying justice for all, unfortunately is neither just nor neutral nor fair. It divided people into make-believe groups, arranged in a hierarchy, in which the upper levels enjoyed power and privilege, and the lower levels suffered discrimination and oppression. The Code of Hammurabi established a pecking order of superiors, commoners and slaves, in which superiors got all the good things in life, the commoners got the rest, and the slaves got a beating if they complained. It has been so throughout the great ancient civilizations. During the 2,000 years of the Christian era, the pecking order endured between the nobility, the priests, the commoners and the heathens. Despite proclamations of equality among men, the Americans of 1776 created a hierarchy between whites who enjoyed liberty and the blacks and the Indian aborigines who did not; also a hierarchy between the rich and the poor, of which liberty simply meant that the state cannot confiscate property without cause or tell the rich what to do with it, and of which equality simply meant laws are applied equally to rich and the poor, which is laughable. In 1776, liberty and equality did not mean the empowerment of the blacks, the Indians and even women in general, to gain and exercise power. Today, our governance and justice systems have improved from empires, dictatorships and caste systems, to modern democracies, from the Code of Hammurabi and the divine Right of Kings, to the French Social Contract and the Rights of Man, and ultimately to the UN Declaration of Human Rights.

But our religions might have not evolved to our liking; our ancient religions based on the mother principle, had many gods in their pantheons but no religious wars; our modern religions based on the Alpha-male Father principle, had one common God – Jehovah, God the Father, and Allah – but their adherents killed each other, sect against sect, church against mosques against synagogues. Christians behaved the worst, worse than the Muslims. Mostly whites and Western Europeans, Christians had internecine wars, wars of conquest, Crusades, Inquisitions that caused the deaths of 700 million in twenty centuries.

This may come as a surprise to you all: the language of numbers antedated the written language, due to the necessity of keeping records on taxes, storage of food and other provisions, and everyday transactions involved in the marketing and exchange of goods. As babies we learn to count before we could write. The first to do this as a people were the ancient Sumerians in southern Mesopotamia, who used clay tablets, stamped with signs for 1, 10, 60, 600, 3,600, and 36,000 – a combination of base-6 and base-10 as a counting system. The base-6 gave us our 24-hour day, 60-minute hour, and 360-degree circle. The Sumerians wanted to write down things other than monotonous numerical data, and added more signs to their system, gradually transforming it to full script called cuneiform. About the same time, the Ancient Egyptians developed a full script known as hieroglyphics. And later, in other parts of the globe, the Chinese in East Asia, and the Incas in South America, developed their own full script of writing. The Romans gave us the alphabet we use today. The Arabic numerals, which was really invented by the Hindus, is the modern mathematical language everyone uses today.

The Agricultural Revolution was a turning point in history 10,000 years ago. At the time of hunters and gathers, covering 2.5 million years of existence, human beings led a better life in intimate symbiosis with nature which provided them with very good diet and an interesting life-style, for at the most, 10 million people. Agriculture provided more food, but an infinitely worse diet, and a dawn-to-dusk dreary life-style for ordinary humans, but caused an exponential growth of population to 250 million by the first century and to 7 billion by the 21st century. For good or ill, there is no turning back. No way can a farming society revert back to hunter-gatherers and provide food for such a population explosion.

But the greatest legacy of the Agricultural Revolution is the development of our free market system. Long ago people at the stage called "subsistence economy" produced only what they needed and had no need for money; but soon production methods improved, people specialized in single products, produced more than they needed, to be exchanged for goods they do not produce. What they needed to have is (1) a store of value and (2) a medium of exchange. They needed to store the value of their surplus production; it is easy to store surplus shoes, but what about surplus perishable goods like vegetables? They needed a way to exchange goods in acceptable units of value everybody trusts; they needed something that is valuable, rare, permanent and non perishable; and they found what everybody wanted, Gold and Silver, which are rare, non-rusting, meltable and ductile, easily made into useful things like utensils, and shining ornaments to win a maiden's heart or enhance a man's sense of importance. People began to make coins of gold and silver in standard units. Thus came into being that wonderful useful thing called MONEY, perfect as a store of value and as a medium of exchange. The very rich found it necessary to build special vaults to hoard their gold and protect them from thieves and robbers; they began to rent out space in their vaults for the storage of gold belonging to others; and became the first "bankers," who issued receipts, for the gold stored. Since gold is very heavy to carry and is a constant temptation for others to rob, such receipts were often used to make purchases, and became the first "paper money." The banker soon noted that while gold was moving in and out of their vaults, there was a lot of gold just sitting there gathering dust. The smart banker then issued receipts for more gold than he actually had in deposits. Today, this is called "creating credit," or making money out of nothing; in olden times, this was considered fraudulent and called for a lynching. Issuing surplus notes is fine, as long as depositors do not ask for their gold all at once. If they did, then the bank had a "run" and depositors would lose their confidence in the Banker, and that would drive him to bankruptcy or to a place of execution. To protect the people from crooked bankers, and also because kings and politicians wanted to have this lucrative racket for themselves, national governments arrogated unto themselves the exclusive right to issue paper money, and this became the paper currency of today.

Humans created artificial instincts that enabled millions of strangers to cooperate effectively. This network of artificial instincts is called "culture". Human cultures are in constant flux, in constant state of change. Is this change completely random, or does it have some overall pattern? In other words, does history have a direction? A bird's eye view of decades and centuries is too myopic. The viewpoint of cosmic spy satellite, scanning millenniums rather than centuries, reveals a crystal-clear view of history moving relentlessly towards unity. For this we credit the greatest conqueror of history, a conqueror possessed of extreme tolerance and adaptability, thereby turning people into ardent disciples. This conqueror is Money, and its most ardent disciples are merchants, conquerors and prophets. For merchants the entire world was a single market, and all humans are potential customers. For conquerors, the entire world is a single kingdom and all humans are potential subjects. For prophets, the entire world holds a single truth and all humans are potential believers. All strive to create a "free market" economic order applicable to everyone everywhere; a universal religion that everyone will believe in, Scientific Atheistic Humanism, under Homo Deus; and an international order of governance based on a Social Contract between the government and the governed, which we now call a Democracy. Predictions don't make it true.

Every point in history is a crossroad where myriad paths fork off into the future. Only 500 years ago, history made its most momentous choice, changing not only the fate of humankind, but arguably the fate of all life on earth. It is the Scientific Revolution; where it leads, we know not.

Chapter 4.
The Scientific Revolution

About 13.5 billion years ago, matter, energy, time and space came into being with the Big Bang, a process we call *physics*; 300,000 years later, matter and energy coalesced into atoms and molecules, a process we call *chemistry*; 3.8 billion years ago, certain molecules combined to form large and intricate organisms, a process we call *biology*; about 70,000 years ago, organisms belonging to Homo Sapiens formed even more intricate structures called *cultures*, a process we call *history*; three important revolutions shaped *history* – the *Cognitive* Revolution which kick-started history 70,000 years ago; the *Agricultural* Revolution sped it up 12,000 years ago; and the *Scientific* Revolution only 500 years ago which may end history, may start something completely different from Homo Sapiens. Thus did a genius named Yuval Noah Harari, of the Jewish race (Semites like their cousins the Arabs, and technically not of the white race), educated in Oxford and not Harvard, summarized his two books, "Sapiens" and "Homo Deus". We wrote of the first two Revolutions, Cognitive and Agricultural. We now write of the third, the Scientific Revolution.

The last 500 years witnessed a phenomenal and unprecedented growth in human power. In the year 1500 AD there were about 500 million human beings in the entire world; today there are 7 billion. The total goods and services produced by humans in year 1500, is estimated to be $250 billion in today's dollars; nowadays the annual value of human production is close to $60 trillion. In the year 1500, humans consumed about 13 trillion calories a day; today we consume 1,500 trillion calories a day. After 500 years, human population increased 14 times; production 240 times; our energy consumption 115 times. In 1522, Magellan's expedition took 3 years to circumnavigate the world, costing the lives of almost all of the crew, including Magellan; today anyone can safely do it in just 2 days. In 1500, humans were confined to the earth's surface, the skies being reserved for birds, angels and gods; on July 20, 1969, for the first time in 4 billion years of evolution, one organism, Sapiens, left our planet Earth and planted his footprint on the moon.

For most of our history we were not aware of the existence of 99.99 % of organisms on our planet, billions of which inhabit each of our bodies, our best friends digesting our food and cleaning our guts, and our deadliest enemies who cause illnesses and epidemics; it was only in 1671 AD when Anton van Leeuwenhoek peered into his home-made microscope and was startled to see an entire world of one-celled creatures milling about in a drop of water; today we engineer bacteria to produce medicines, manufacture biofuel, and kill parasites. But the single most remarkable and defining moment of the past 500 years came at exactly 05:29:45 on the morning of July 16, 1945 when scientists detonated the first atomic bomb at Alamogordo, New Mexico, giving mankind the capability not only to change the course of history, but to end it. This historical process that led to New Mexico and to the moon is known as the Scientific Revolution.

It all started with the Discovery of Ignorance. Modern science is built on the Latin injunction *ignoramus*, meaning "we do not know." It assumes that we do not know everything, that the things we know to be true could be proven wrong as we gain more knowledge. No concept, idea or theory is sacred and beyond challenge. Admitting ignorance, science seeks to obtain new knowledge, by gathering observations and using mathematical tools to connect observations to theories, then using such theories to acquire new powers and develop new technologies.

In 1687, Isaac Newton explained all movements of all bodies in the universe from canon balls to shooting stars, in three simple laws: (1) an object either remains at rest or continues to move at a constant velocity, unless acted upon by an outside force; (2) vector sum of the forces $\mathbf{F}$ on an object is equal to the mass m of that object multiplied by the acceleration $\mathbf{a}$ of the object: $\mathbf{F} = m\mathbf{a}$; (3) When one body exerts a force on a second body, the second body simultaneously exerts a force equal in magnitude and opposite in direction on the first body.

In the past, Theological Truth was explained by narratives like those of the Bible and Koran. Isaac Newton showed that the Book of Science and Nature is written in the language of Mathematics, and he invented a new branch of math called *Calculus*, to explain change: *the derivative of x with respect to y is equal to the increment of x divided by the increment of y as the increment of y approaches zero*, which is used to explain how a line becomes an angle, becomes a triangle, becomes a rectangle, becomes a polygon, and eventually becomes a circle as the number of sides approaches infinity. Physics, astronomy, chemistry, quantum mechanics, can be reduced to clear-cut equations, but not biology, economics, and psychology which are much too complex. Mathematicians don't give up, they invented a new branch of mathematics called *Statistics* subject to the laws of probabilities, to analyze trends, patterns, permutations and combinations of human behavior in these complex fields.

In 1687 Isaac Newton wrote *Mathematical Principles of Natural Philosophy,* one of the most important books in the history of modern science. In 1744, two Presbyterian clergymen in Scotland, Alexander Webster and Robert Wallace did not consult the Bible, instead contacted a professor of mathematics Colin MacLaurin to devise a life insurance fund that would provide pensions for widow and orphans of dead clergymen, based on statistics of income, investment and life expectancy. In 1776, another Scot, Adam Smith, a moral philosopher, did not consult the Bible either; he used the scientific method to write *The Wealth of Nations* by which pursuit of self interest and the division of labor would result in the best interests of all, the most important work in Economics. In 1859, Charles Darwin, who studied to be an Anglican clergyman, did not consult the Bible either, rejected the Genesis story, and wrote *On the Origin of Species*, with compelling evidence of his theory of Evolution that all life evolved over long periods of time, based on the process of natural selection and the survival of the fittest – the most important work in the field of Biology. It was in England that the Industrial Revolution happened. We had many sources of energy but we did not know how to convert one type of energy to another; we used wind to move sails but not to heat water; the only energy-conversion devices were Sapiens and animals who can convert food to muscle power to do many varied tasks. In 1765 James Watt re-invented the steam engine to use heat from coal to generate steam that can move pistons to power pumps to keep water out of coal mines, to power locomotives to transport people and goods at long distance, and eventually to power machines to manufacture textiles and other products. In a few years, England had railroads more than the rest of the world, and became the world's first industrial power.

Why England, followed quickly by France, Germany and United States, and not China or India which together at the time, represented two-thirds of the economy of the world? Why the British Isles and Western Europe, the distant backwaters of the Roman Empire which considered then a poor Wild West, so desolate and barbarous that they were not even worth conquering? But between

1500 and 1750, western Europe became a hothouse of important military, political, economic and cultural developments that gained momentum to become master of the "Outer World", meaning the two American continents and the oceans. Even then, Europe was no match for the great powers of Asia. Europeans managed to conquer America and gained supremacy at sea mainly because the Asiatics showed little interest in them.

A few years before, Admiral Zheng He of the Ming Dynasty eclipsed European voyages of discovery with ships (120 meters long) that dwarfed Columbus' ships (26 meters long); but Zheng did not conquer and colonize, and his fleet was dismantled and destroyed, because it was expensive to maintain, and because Chinese were not interested in bullying other countries. England and Western Europe prevailed because its Scientific Revolution worked hand in hand with Imperialism and Capitalism.

We wrote of the first bankers issuing receipts for gold deposits that do not exist, making money out of nothing, a process called "creating credit". Modern banking does the same thing in a massive way. Economics is a notoriously complicated subject, but let us imagine a simple example. Let's say Henry Sy opens a new bank Banco de Oro. David Consunji opens a business of construction, earns profit from his first big job and makes a deposit of P1 million cash in BDO, Sy's bank, which now has P1 million in capital. A third person, William Belo wants to construct a building for his new business, Wilcon Depot, for the marketing of hardware, but he does not have enough capital, so he borrows P1 million cash from BDO, and pays it to David Consunji for building his facility. David deposits this P1 million in BDO. David therefore has P2 million in BDO, but how much cash is actually inside the vaults of BDO? Only P1 million, right? This is only the beginning. Two months later, David informs William that due to unforeseen circumstances, the Wilcon facility will eventually cost P2 million; William is annoyed, but he cannot stop the job in the middle, so he borrows another P1 million, hands it over to David who deposits it in Henry's Bank. This time, David has P3 million in his account, but how much cash is sitting in Henry's Bank? Still the same P1 million that has been there from the beginning!!

The Central Bank system, as well as the US Federal Reserve system, allows this process to be repeated several times. Banks are allowed to lend as much as P10 for every P1 dollar of deposit, so that 90% of the money in bank accounts is not covered by actual coins and paper currency. Sounds like a fraudulent Ponzi scheme, but it is not. If all the depositors demand to have their money back, the bank will promptly collapse, and the depositor will lose their savings, but chances are, the government will save the bank by lending it the needed cash, and guaranteeing reimbursement to the depositors. This whole system is not a deception but a tribute to the amazing abilities of the human imagination. What enables banks and the entire economy to survive and flourish is our Trust in the Future. This Trust is the sole backing of all the money in the world.

The discrepancy between David's bank account of P3 million and the P1 million in Henry's bank vault, is reflected in William's P2 million worth of assets in Wilcon Depot. William has not sold a single article of hardware, but Henry's bank trusts him to do good business and eventually generate enough profits to pay the bank P2 million plus interest. So that if David wants to withdraw his P3 million deposit, he can do so without ruining the bank. The entire enterprise is thus founded on Trust in an imaginary Future – the Trust that William Belo has in the Future of his business, along with David's Trust in the Future solvency of Henry's bank.

Unlimited credit, money made out nothing, is made available to generate economic Growth during the Scientific era. In the past, no such credit was available because bankers did not trust the future. During the Agriculture era, economics was a zero-sum game, per capita production and the size of the economic pie remained the same, so that the wealthy became wealthier by making the poor even poorer. That is why Jesus said that it is easier for camels to go through the eye of a needle than a rich man's chance to enter heaven. He assumes that the rich extort their wealth from the poor. That is no longer true during the modern scientific era. Capitalism makes a distinction between wealth and capital: wealth is for conspicuous consumption; capital is for investment in the Future. Wealth is for kings and nobles and festivities and fine clothes and unproductive things. Capital is for shopkeepers and bankers and board chairmen in inconspicuous suits and machines and labor and raw materials and things that are productive for the benefit of the human race.

For the last 500 years, the idea of unlimited growth and progress, and ever larger economic pie took hold, credit ballooned into large, long-term, low-interest loans, exceeding current income. Unlimited power – wind, solar, nuclear, biogas – gave us prosperity beyond our wildest dreams!

How far is it from the Sun to the Earth? The only way to answer this was to take advantage of the passage of planet Venus between the Sun and the Earth which happens every few years; the duration of the transit differs when seen from distant points on the earth's surface because of the tiny difference in the angle at which the observer sees it. If several observations of the transit were made from different continents, simple trigonometry was all it would take to calculate our exact distance from the sun. Astronomers predicted that the next Venus transits would occur in 1761 and 1769. In 1761, scientists observed the transit from Siberia, North America, Madagascar and Africa. As the 1769 transit approached, the European community mounted a supreme effort, and scientists were sent as far north as Canada and California. The Royalty Society of London for the Improvement of Natural Knowledge concluded that this was not enough. To obtain the most accurate results, it was imperative to send an astronomer all the way to the southwestern Pacific Ocean. The Royal Society resolved to send an eminent astronomer Charles Green, to Tahiti, and spared no expense, but it made no sense to spend all that money for just one single astronomical observation. So the Society sent a Royal Navy ship under the command of Captain James Cook, along with Green, 8 other scientists of different disciplines, and artists, headed by two botanists, Joseph Banks and Daniel Solander. Captain James Cook, an experienced seaman as well as an accomplished geographer, brought with him 85 well-armed sailors and marines and equipped the ship with artillery, muskets, gunpowder, and other weaponry, and instead of biscuits and beef jerky, loaded up with sauerkraut and instructions for his crew to eat a lot of fresh fruits and vegetables whenever the ship made landfall. This marriage of Science, Capitalism and Imperialism bore many fruits: (1) the distance between the the sun and our earth was computed as 149.6 million km; (2) it brought back enormous quantities of astronomical, geographical, meteorological, botanical, zoological and anthropological data, complete with accurate drawings that sparked the interest of Europeans with astonishing tales of the South Pacific, and inspired future generations of scientists, naturalists and astronomers; (3) the Cook nautical diet of citrus fruits full of Vitamin C, cured scurvy which caused the deaths of countless sailors and passengers in the past, and contributed greatly to British control of the world's oceans; (4) it laid the foundation of British occupation and conquest of Australia, Tasmania and New Zealand, for the settlement of Europeans in the new colonies, and for the cruel extermination of large animals and most of the aborigines.

Science, Capitalism, and Imperialism enabled the British to set up themselves up as masters of all the seas and lords of lands upon which the sun never set, carrying their "white man's burden" to civilize the world. By sheer force of arms, they took the riches of India and China, which at the time together produced two-thirds of the world's wealth – incorporating India into its vast empire, deliberately poisoning the Chinese people with opium, which led to the demise of the oldest surviving civilization of the human race, that existed for 4,000 years and coexisted with Ancient Egypt. They occupied the continent of Australia, New Zealand and Tasmania, and massacred all but a few of the native populations. These British Imperialists and Capitalists did not spare their own people, as Charles Dickens depicted in his novels. The British contemptuously referred to their predecessor imperialists, the darker Spaniards, Italians and the Greeks as "greasers", the French as "frogs" and the Jews as "kikes". The British and their Aryan cousins, the Dutch, the Germans and the Americans, developed notions of racial superiority and wreaked havoc in West and South Africa (supply of slaves and the apartheid regime), Indonesia (the cruel exploitation of the East Indies), the Philippines (the Samar Massacre of men, women and children down to 10 years old, and the CIA Low-Intensity-Conflict), North and South America (slavery of blacks and genocide of Indians, United Fruit Co.), the Middle East (for fuel oil) and the rest of the world.

The last 500 years have witnessed our earth united into a single ecological and historical sphere; the economy growing exponentially, producing wealth of the stuff of fairy tales; science giving humankind superhuman powers and practically limitless energy.

Both our gurus, Yuval Noah Harari and Steven Pinker predict that the world of the future will ideally be governed on the basis of Reason, Science and Enlightenment. Pinker imagines this to be Scientific Atheistic Humanism whose aim is Liberty and whose values are liberal, that is, based on the sanctity of human life. But Harari goes further and says that Humanism is not one, but three: one of USA and Western Europe whose main aim is liberty, another from the Socialist world whose main aim is equality, and still another whose roots are in Germany whose main aim is the survival-of-the-fittest. Indeed, life, liberty and equality are the highest aspirations of

Sapiens. But Harari says that biology has proven that equality and liberty are illusions, that we evolved with characteristics that make us different, not equal, that we are free to act only as our feelings, neurons and genome dictate; that survival-of-the-fittest is the one and only law that has governed evolution of all creatures including ours. He gives us a scenario of the future.

The sanctity of life was enshrined because men have value as voters in the political process, because men turn the wheels of industry, because men man the machines of war. That is not necessarily so in the near future. Because of the nuclear bomb, all-out war is collective suicide and will be avoided, any war today will be fought not by humans but by drones and sophisticated weapons that need only a finger to activate. Robots that are more efficient and accurate will displace men in the assembly line. And computer algorithms will eventually govern all human activities: Waze with Google's driverless cars will manage the traffic systems; Watson algorithms will displace diagnosis of doctors; algorithms like Facebook's and Google's that will know us more than we know ourselves, may be trusted to replace human decision and action in every human endeavor. Man's ability to read and manipulate the DNA code, gives him the power to control all Evolution, including his own, to elevate Sapiens to the next stage – Homo Deus, not like Jehovah, but something like the Greek Gods, enhanced Humans with godlike powers. The digital revolution is preparing the world for Project Zero of Unlimited Abundance, its aims being zero carbon energy system, the production of products, machines and services with zero marginal costs, and reduction of necessary labor time as close as possible to zero. Already we are the benefits of "free stuff" that has made obsolete the post office, libraries, landlines, photographic films, cameras, etc.

Our evolution, according to Harari, naturally will proceed as it always did, driven by survival-of-the-fittest, with an enhanced individuals controlling algorithms, robots and drones and other instruments of power, to provide "useless and pampered" masses what they need to enjoy life. Who will we trust to chart our future? Obviously a group of people of science and with talent for organization. Three come to mind: the Jews who are the brightest in the planet, the Chinese who are arguably the second brightest and best organized, and the Americans, the strongest and the most technologically advanced. If the Jews can be the tail that wags the

American dog, as they are in the Middle East, it is a cinch the Americans will be our masters. The Americans, like the rest of the Germanic races, with notions of racial superiority, are too cruel and too greedy, and may treat the lower classes, as Harari predicts, like Indians and farm animals. Americans are vengeful, reacting totally out of proportion to alleged slights: 130,000 civilian deaths by atom bomb, as a reaction to 2,300 sailors dead in Pearl Harbor; 50,000 deaths down to 10 years of age in Samar, as a reaction to 50 soldiers ambushed in Balangiga; 1 million Iraqis dead as a reaction to 3,500 victims on 9/11. I believe we're better off entrusting our future to the oldest surviving civilization of people with no notions of racial superiority, who absorbed and civilized their conquerors, who never occupied lands outside their borders.

Chapter 5.
Human Relationship with Animals

The key to understanding our history and psychology as the genus Homo, is to realize the until only recently, our position in the food chain was solidly in the middle. Since we evolved 2.5 million years ago, we humans were animals of no significance, hunting small animals and while being hunted by large predators. We humans had large brains which at rest consumed 25% of our energy, while most animals' brains at rest consumed only 8% of their energy. Like societies that prioritize education rather that military expenditures, we remained weak; we can win an argument with orangutans, but they can tear us apart like rag dolls.

But in the end, our investment in brain power paid off. It was only 400,000 years ago that several species of humans (including the Neanderthals) began to hunt large game on a regular basis, and only in the last 100,000 years, with the rise of Homo Sapiens (which in a Cognitive Revolution, 70,000 years ago, acquired special skills in communication with and acting in cooperation with large numbers of strangers) did man jumped to the top of the food chain.

The dog was the first animal domesticated by man, some 15,000 years ago. The dog is truly man's best friend, useful in hunting and fighting, and as an alarm system against wild beasts and human intruders. With each passing generation dog and man co-evolved with deep understanding and affection for each other, that exists to this day, unique in the annals of mankind.

In true feline form, cats took their time deciding whether to jump into humans' laps; we did not domesticate them, they domesticated themselves. The cats likely started hanging around farming communities in the Fertile Crescent about 8,000 years ago, where they settled into a mutually beneficial relationship as humans' rodent patrol, the first recorded being an Egyptian cat mummy. The blotched or striped coat markings of tabby cats appeared in the Middle Ages; only in the 18th century, were the markings became common enough to be associated with domestic cats, and in the 19th century, did cat fanciers begin selecting cats with particular traits to create fancy breeds.

Rodents comprise one of the 16 orders of mammals. Of its 31 families, the most successful is the *Murididae*, and of its several genera, the most prolific is the *Rattus*, which has at least 570 species -- but only two of these have become Man's reluctant partners and greatest enemies: *Rattus rattus* (the black rat), and *Rattus norvegicus* (the brown rat). These two, with their cousin, *Mus musculus* (house mouse), account for practically half of the animal population on earth, and are the unwanted guests of man in the very house he lives in. The rat discovered that a man's house is a nice place to live in, despite his lack of hospitality. The host builds drains and sewers for commuting, and fills them with kitchen refuse and toilet waste for rats to share with cockroaches. In the conflict between Man and Rat, the score is almost even, with the rats perhaps a trifle ahead. There are now 7 billion humans on this planet, most of whom are wretched and underfed. There are also 7 billion rats and mice, but most of them are comparatively well-fed and comfortable in our houses, drains and fields. The relationship between man and rat is a comparative recent affair. The ancient Greek and Romans wrote about the mouse, but never mentioned the rat.

The rat is a native of our part of the world, Southeast Asia, and the first of them to reach Europe was the Black Rat (*Rattus rattus*) which took thousands of years to migrate house by house, village by village, across India, the Middle East and North Africa. The rise of the city 50 centuries ago and the appearance of sailing ships bound for distant shores broadened the ambitions of the Black Rat. The Crusaders, from the 11th to the 14th centuries, brought the Black Rat across the Mediterranean to Europe on their ships. And there in Europe the Black Rat promptly infected the population with the bubonic plague (Black Death) which in three years claimed 25 million lives, one fourth of the population of Europe.

In the year 1727, Russian serfs along the Volga River reported thousands upon thousands of rats of a strange new breed swimming across the river. At last the Brown Rat had broken out of its Asian stronghold and embarked on its conquest of the world. What took the Black Rat thousands of years to do, took the Brown Rat only 125 years to accomplish. Within the first three years, the Brown Rat was in England and in 1755 it was in North America, more than two hundred years after the Black Rat crossed the Atlantic Ocean in 1540. By the 1850s, the Brown Rat's mission was complete. It now infests every part of the world, from the tundras of Alaska to the banks of the

Amazon and the Congo, from the subways of New York to the fjords of Scandinavia, from the Australian outback to the rice fields of Mindanao. The triumph of the Brown Rat naturally brought it face to face with the Black Rat. It was no contest. When Black meets Brown, the Black backs off. The belligerent Brown arrives upon the scene, surveys the accommodations and orders its Black occupants out. Since Browns feel more at home close to the ground and blacks are content with the heights, a happy compromise is worked out. The rats scurrying all over the ceiling are Blacks, those burrowing under the kitchen floor are Browns. The boundary line is drawn on the stairs.

Man has lately been hitting below the belt in his duel with the rat. He has been assembling an arsenal of poisons, gases, acids, electrocution chambers and ultrasonic vibrations that kill up to 90 percent of the rats in one search and destroy mission.

Mother Nature must love rats, because to compensate for their lack of Einsteins and Edisons, she gave rats an instinct that enshrines genetically in every cell a faultless understanding of Darwin's Natural Selection, Pavlov's Conditioned Reflex, and Malthus' Principle of Population Growth. In a campaign of rat extermination, up to 90 percent of the rat population are killed. But the survivors are not determined by chance. It is always the smartest 10 percent that avoid being killed, learning fast which places are dangerous and which morsels contain the rat poison. It is always the dumb ones who find out too late. Thus the mass extermination of rats ensures that only the cleverest survive to breed a new generation. The more effective the killing, the sharper grows the instinctive intelligence encoded in the genes of those which live to mate. Super rat-killers may be breeding super-rats. And someday these critters are going to outsmart the human race.

Female humans begin their sex life at 12 years old, and can only bear one child every nine months. Each female rat begins its sex life at 3 months old, has a litter of eight babies every seven weeks; and can theoretically have 128 million descendants in three years, at which time she becomes senile, feeble and barren. So the final question: Why the rat and not the beaver or the hairy nosed wombat? One may well ask why man evolved as the master species, and not the dolphin or the orangutan.

The answer would be the same: the lack of specialization presents the race with a stark choice -- adaptation or extinction. Thousands of other species too specialized to adapt had died out -- the dinosaur, sabertooth, dodo bird. Only through the goodwill and sufferance of man do the rest of the animals survive -- the elephant, lion, whale, monkey-eating eagle.

Only the rat survives the hatred, enmity and all-out war by Man. Perhaps on the last few days on earth, there will be only two creatures left to contest the mastery of our planet -- Man and the only enemy he never conquered, the Rat.

In a dramatic foretaste of the way the world would end, nuclear tests conducted by the United States in the Eniwetok Atoll rocked the Engebi islet with blinding explosions and fierce fire storms -- gouging out mammoth craters, vaporizing all life and vegetation, engulfing all land with cataclysmic tidal waves and palls of lethal radiation beneath tell-tale mushroom clouds. A few years later, biologists visited the little island. They found the island still radioactive and barren of life -- except for a large colony of rats, not maimed or genetically deformed creatures, but robust rodents whose life spans were longer than average.

How about the sheep, goats, pigs and chickens on which humans preyed for food, how were they domesticated? This process probably began with selective hunting. First, humans learned the advantage of killing only adult rams and old and dying sheep, and sparing fertile females and young lambs to preserve the vitality of the herd. Second was to actively defend the herd from lions, wolves and other humans, driving the herd into narrow gorges to better control and defend it. Finally, humans learned to selectively control them to tailor them to human needs, killing first, the most aggressive rams who resist control, together with skinny and inquisitive females who tend to wander away, so that with each passing generation, the sheep came fatter and more submissive.

Alternatively, humans may have captured and adopted a lamb, and fattened it for slaughter in leaner times. At some stage, they keep a greater number of these lambs, some of which would reach puberty and procreate. The most aggressive and unruly lambs are killed first, and the most submissive allowed to procreate. These domesticated sheep, along with domesticated chickens, cattle, goats and pigs, supplied food (meat, milk, eggs), raw materials (skin, wool) and muscle power for transportation, plowing, grinding and other tasks hitherto performed by human sinews.

As humans spread around the world, so did their domesticated animals. 10,000 years ago, not more than a few million sheep, cattle, goats, pigs and chickens lived in a restricted Afro-Asian niches. Today the world contains about a billion sheep, a billion pigs, more than a billion cattle, and more that 25 billion chickens. The domesticated chicken is the most widespread fowl ever. The humans and the rats (and mice) are equally the most widespread and numerous of all mammals, followed by domesticated farm animals enumerated above, then Cats, and then Dogs which are apparently less popular as pets than cats.

The domestication of farm animals was founded on a series of brutal practices that only became more cruel with the passage of time. The natural lifespan of chickens is about 7 to 12 years, and that of cattle from 20 to 25 years, but a vast majority of domesticated chickens and cattle are slaughtered at the age of a few weeks and few months, because this is the optimal slaughtering age from an economic perspective. Why keep feeding a cock for three years when it has already reached its maximum weight after three months? Egg-laying hens, milking cows and draft animals are allowed to live for many years, under subjugation completely alien to their urges and desires. Instead of being allowed to wander over open prairies in the company of their fellow creatures, cows are forced to pull carts and plowshares under the whip. Farmers developed such techniques as locking them up on pens and cages, bridling them in harnesses and leashes, training them with whips and cattle prods, and even castrating them to restrain male aggression, and to selectively control procreation.

The dairy industry has its own ways of forcing animals to do its will. Cows, goats and sheep only produce milk after giving birth, and only as long as their youngsters are suckling. The most common method was simply to slaughter the calves, kids and lambs shortly after birth, milk the mother for all she's worth, and get her pregnant again. In many modern farms, a milk cow is allowed to live 5 years before being slaughtered. During those five years she is almost constantly pregnant, and is fertilized within 60 to 120 days after giving birth to preserve maximum milk production. Her calves are separated from her shortly after birth. The females are reared to become the next generation of dairy cows, while the males are handed over to the care of the meat industry.

Not all agricultural societies are cruel to their farm animals. The lives of some domesticated animals could be quite good. Sheep raised for wool, pet dog and cats, war horses and race horses often enjoy comfortable conditions. Yet from the viewpoint of the herd, rather than that of a shepherd, it is hard not to conclude that the Agricultural Revolution was a terrible catastrophe.

William Jennings Bryan, 3-time US Presidential Candidate and head of the Anti-Imperialist League opposing the colonization of the Philippines, faced eminent lawyer Clarence Darrow in the famous "Scopes Monkey Trial" in Tennessee on an issue that involved the teaching of Darwinian evolution in American schools. Bryan who was a Christian Fundamentalist, argued that as a Christian nation, the USA is committed to the Biblical version of the origin of Man and the Universe, which only an Intelligent Design by a Creator can make possible. Darrow argued that Evolution is not inconsistent with Christianity, that as his followers believe, science and reason dictate that Darwin was right.

For close to 4 billion years, every single organism on the planet evolved blindly and randomly according to natural selection and survival of the fittest; not a single one was designed by an intelligent creator. Intelligent Design versus Random Evolution. In Tennessee in 1925, Intelligent Design won, and the teacher who taught Evolution was fined $100.00. Subsequently the US Courts ruled that nobody really won, that because of the separation of church and state, everyone is free to teach what he personally believes in.

In reality everybody actually won, because today in 2018, while Darwinian Evolution is true in the past 4 billion years, by virtue of Homo Sapiens' ability to read and rewrite the DNA genetic code, Man is on the threshold of employing Intelligent Design to control the evolution of life.

Eduardo Kac, a Brazilian bio-artist, commissioned a French laboratory to engineer a radiant bunny according to his specifications. The French scientists took an ordinary white rabbit embryo, implanted in its DNA a gene taken from a green fluorescent jellyfish, and created one green fluorescent rabbit for Mr. Kac who named the rabbit Alba.

It is impossible to explain the existence of Alba through the laws of natural selection; she is a product of intelligent design, a harbinger of things to come, a sign that the Scientific Revolution may turn out to the the most important biological revolution since the appearance of life on earth. After 4 billion years of Natural Selection, Alba stands at the dawn of a new cosmic era, in which life will be ruled by Intelligent Design. This can happen in three ways, through:

(1) biological engineering, (2) cyborg engineering (cyborgs are beings that combine organic with non-organic parts, (4) or the engineering of inorganic life.

Alba is an example of biological engineering, implanting a gene to modify an organism to a preconceived result. On quite another level, humans have castrated aggressive bulls to create submissive oxen, castrated young human males to create soprano voices, and eunuchs to be entrusted with the care of a sultan's harem, to change his sex through surgical and hormonal treatments.

But imagine the surprise, disgust and consternation that ensued when in 1996, a newspaper photo showed a mouse on whose back scientists grew an ear made of cattle cartilage ears! This raised a host of ethical issues and the prevailing feeling that too many opportunities are opening too quickly and that our ability to modify genes is outpacing our capacity to make wise decisions. We are haunted by apocalyptic visions of bio-dictatorships that will clone fearless soldiers and obedient workers or supermen who will make serfs of the rest of us. As a result, we are using only a fraction of the potential of genetic engineering, concentrating on organisms with the weakest political lobbies: plants, fungi, bacteria and insects, creating bacteria to produce biofuel and cheap insulin, extracting a gene from an Arctic fish, to make potatoes more frost-resistant.

Today scientists are engaged in engineering cows whose milk contain lysostaphin that attacks bacteria causing mastitis, which attacks milk cow udders; pigs implanted with a gene from a worm that will convert unhealthy pork fat (omega 6) to good ones (omega 3); in engineering worms with a six-fold increase in life-expectancy, and in engineering genius mice with a much improved memory and learning skills, raising hopes for doing the same thing for humans.

Voles are small rodents resembling mice, mostly promiscuous as Filipino actor-politicians, except for one species that have lasting and monogamous relationships similar to that displayed by Opus Dei super-numeraries like Jose Cuisia, Placido Mapa Jr. and Francisco Tatad, and their wives. Scientists claim that they have isolated the genes responsible for vole monogamy, and they have used this gene to turn Casanova voles into loyal and loving mates. Are we far off from doing the same to humans, turning actor Ramon Revilla into a Jose Cuisia, and changing the entire social marriage structure of humankind? God forbid, President Rodrigo Duterte may say.

Geneticists do not only want to transform living creatures, they want to revive extinct creatures as well. A team of Russian, Japanese and Korean scientists has recently mapped the genome of ancient mammoths found frozen in the Siberian ice, plan to fertilize the egg of an elephant, replace the elephantine DNA with the reconstructed mammoth DNA, implant the egg in the womb of an elephant, and wait for about 22 months for the birth of first mammoth to be born in 5,000 years! Are we far off from expecting dinosaurs to roam in our own Jurassic Park?

Why stop at mammoths? Professor George Church of Harvard University suggests that with the completion of the Neanderthal Genome Project, we can now implant reconstructed Neanderthal DNA into a Sapiens ovum, producing the first Neanderthal child in 30,000 years. Several women have already volunteered as surrogate mothers. By comparing the Neanderthal brain to that of Sapiens brain, and mapping out where their structures differ, perhaps we can find out what biological changes produced consciousness as we experience it, and why the Neanderthal ceased to exist and why we survived. There is an ethical reason too – if we Sapiens were responsible for the demise of our cousins the Neanderthals, it is our moral duty to resurrect them.

Why stop at Neanderthals? As Professor Yuval Noah Harari suggests, why not go back to God's drawing board, and design a better Homo Sapiens? The abilities, needs and desires of Homo Sapiens have a genetic base. And the Sapiens genome is no more complex than that of voles and mice. The mouse genome contains about 2.5 billion nucleobases; the Sapiens genome about 2.9 billion bases – a mere 14% larger. In a few decades, genetic engineering and other forms of biological engineering might enable us to make far-reaching alterations not only to our physiology, immune system and life expectancy, but also to our intellectual and emotional capacities. If genetic engineering can create genius mice, why not genius humans? If it can create monogamous voles, why not humans hard-wired to be to remain faithful to their partners?

The Cognitive Revolution that has turned Homo Sapiens from an insignificant ape to the master of the world, did not require any noticeable change in the physiology or even the size or external shape of his brain. It apparently involved no more than a few small changes to the internal brain structure. Perhaps another small change would be enough to ignite a Second Cognitive Revolution, to create a completely new type of consciousness, and transform Homo Sapiens into something altogether different and superior.

True we do not have acumen to achieve this. But there seems to be no insurmountable technical barrier preventing us from producing superhumans. The main obstacles are the ethical and political objections that have slowed down research on humans. And no matter how convincing ethical arguments may be, it is hard to see how they can hold back the next step for long, especially if what is at stake is prolonging human life indefinitely, conquering incurable diseases, develop a cure for Alzheimer's that will also grant super-memories to healthy people.

It is unclear whether bioengineering can resurrect the Neanderthal. But it is most likely to bring down the curtain on Sapiens. Tinkering with our genes may not necessarily kill us. But we may fiddle with Homo Sapiens to such extent that we would no longer be Homo Sapiens.

Chapter 6.
Homo Deus, "a brief history of tomorrow"

Since time immemorial, the main preoccupation of mankind was famine, plague and war. Men prayed to every god, invented countless tools, institutions and social systems, and still died in the millions from hunger, epidemics and violence. Thinkers and prophets concluded that famine, plague and war must be an integral part of God's cosmic plan.

At the dawn of the third millennium, however, man wakes up and realizes that since the second half of the 20th century, famine, plagues and war are no longer uncontrollable threats to life. For the first time ever, more people die from eating too much than from eating too little, more people die from old age than from infectious diseases, and more people commit suicide than are killed by soldiers, terrorists and criminals combined. Today the average Filipino is more likely to die of eating junk food at Jollibee, than from drought, malaria, and assassination, all put together.

Since famine, plague and war have become manageable challenges, what will be next on the agenda of mankind? Success breeds ambition. Having reduced mortality from starvation, disease and violence – having achieved unprecedented levels of prosperity, health and harmony -- humanity's next targets are more likely to be <u>immortality, happiness and divinity</u>.

Immortality? Why not? Ever since the dawn of time, we have searched for the Fountain of Eternal Youth. When that proved improbable, we imagined we have an eternal soul so we may live in heaven for all time. Today our philosophers say we have a right to life, and our scientists act on the assumption that it has no expiry date; they keep on extending and extending it beyond all expectations, to delay or even defeat death, and even plan to freeze our bodies to survive centuries of travel to distant stars. The breakneck development of genetic engineering, regenerative medicine and nanotechnology fosters optimistic prophecies.

Happiness? Of course! Life and liberty may be guaranteed by the Constitution, but not happiness. What is guaranteed is the *pursuit* of happiness! But happiness alas is elusive, fleeting and very temporary, and unhappily, human beings are not built for lasting happiness. For happiness is born of the realization of great expectations, and expectations bloom faster than realizations do. One job promotion produces happiness temporarily, one orgasm produces pleasure momentarily; but the pursuit of promotions can only lead to ultimate frustration, and the pursuit of orgasms can only lead to exhaustion and ultimate boredom.

Science tells us that pleasure only comes with the stimulation of certain parts of the brain. And lasting pleasure can only be achieved by electrodes inserted in the brain (as in laboratory rats) or smoking tobacco or marijuana or using illegal drugs, as humans do, although the government discourages and forbids it. But why? Because such pursuit of pleasure, ultimately affects our health and our usefulness. But science is not giving up. More drugs like Valium and Viagra are being produced that will enhance our happiness without being addictive or deleterious to our health. And someday robots will replace workers, smart drones and nuclear power will replace soldiers and prevent war, driverless cars will displace chauffeurs, computers and algorithms will displace doctors, postal workers, librarians – till at last most humans will be rendered useless and pampered, and may be allowed to use drugs in lasting bliss.

Divinity, certainly! Not like the omnipotent Christian God or Jehovah, but more like the Greek and Roman gods, who are more like enhanced human beings, with human faults and frailties, but endowed with far greater power. Already modern man has outstripped his ancient gods: he plows through and under the heaving oceans, sweeps the virgin heights, moves mountains, and bores through earth and rocks. He sends his merest whisper around the world, and conquers time and timeless space. He multiplies loaves and fishes in far greater quantities, rescues more people from death, achieves virgin birth and creates new life in vitro, manipulates his own evolution, and walks on air through air hoses. Truly godlike, he worships himself as Homo Deus.

Chapter 7.
Computer algorithms, our master

An algorithm is defined as a methodical set of steps that can be used to make calculations, resolve problems and reach decisions. Mathematics, algebra, calculus are all algorithms. And so are all living organisms, flora and fauna. A baboon yearning to pick a fruit from a tree with lion lurking nearby, calculates through his instincts and sensations, his chances of success: if he is starving, he might take a chance; if he is not hungry, risking his life may not be worth the effort.

Mankind is the master race of Planet Earth, because the human being is the best algorithm: he has the highest intelligence coupled with the most developed consciousness, so that he can not only play chess, drive cars, diagnose diseases and identify terrorists, but he can also write poetry, compose symphonies and contemplate the mysteries of the universe. But then digital technology and the computer came into being, with its ability to make billions of calculations in one second of time, detecting patterns of behavior, analyzing trends, even recognizing faces, charting a different approach to super-intelligence, without the consciousness to feel emotion.

Which is then more important, intelligence or consciousness? The answer is that as far as armies and corporations are concerned, intelligence is mandatory, but consciousness is optional.

Take our system of transportation. A taxi driver while driving, may enjoy listening to music and gaze in awe as he looks at the stars, but the system does not really care, because its job is bringing the car from Point A to Point B, as quickly, safely and cheaply as possible. And if Google's and Tesla's driverless car can do this far better than a human driver can, then we should use the driverless car, even if it cannot enjoy music or the magic of existence. Remember that an ordinary horse can smell, love, recognize faces, jump over fences and do a thousand things better than a Model T Ford or a modern Rolls Royce. But cars replaced horses because they are superior in the few tasks that the system needed. Taxi drivers will likely suffer the fate of horses.

In a long experimental phase, human drivers were involved in several accidents while Google's driverless cars never suffered an accident except once, it was bumped by a careless human driver. The study concluded that this could not happen if ALL vehicles were connected to an integrated computer system, controlled by one algorithm, which will prevent collision of driverless cars. Reason dictates that to save time, money and human lives, we give computer algorithms monopoly over traffic, and cause the bankruptcy of Toyota, GM and car industries.

Computer algorithms will eventually (1) take over as all-knowing oracles, (2) evolve as agents and (3) finally rule as sovereigns of the human race. Take Waze, the algorithm that is constantly updated about traffic jams, car accidents and police cars, and which suggests ways to avoid traffic, and the quickest possible route.

As an "oracle," it suggests, and you decide whether to follow or not. But when you trust it enough, the logical step is to appoint it as your "agent," even as you couple it to Google's self-driving car; you give your final destination and tell Waze to take the quickest route, or the most scenic route possible. You call the shots, and as your agent, it executes your order.

Finally, Waze may eventually become your "sovereign," your lord and master, which manipulates you and others, shaping your desires and making decisions without consulting you. Suppose there is a traffic jam on route no. 1, while route no. 2 is relatively open. If Waze tells everybody that, all will rush to route no. 2, and soon it too will be clogged. So Waze makes its decision, it tells half the drivers to move to route no. 2, without telling the other half, so route no. 1 will ease the traffic without clogging route no. 2. If everybody uses the same oracle, and everyone trusts the oracle, then the oracle becomes our sovereign, our lord and master.

What is true for the transportation, is true for all. Computer algorithms (like IMB's Watson) will displace doctors; will displace stock-market analysts, lawyers and paralegals, sport referees, cashiers, waiters, tour guides, security guards, etcetera. Human beings are destined to be useless, redundant… and pampered.

Chapter 8.
Is God necessary?

Comes now Doctor of Psychology Steven Pinker of Harvard, whose 8 books elicited praise from Bill Gates ("most inspiring I ever read") and from London Times, New York Times and Time magazine ("sweeping, erudite, sharply argued, fun to read, highly persuasive"), asking: Is God really necessary? Do we need God to tell us what is right or wrong, what is good or bad, in other words, to establish a code of morals that allow us to live with each other in peace as befits human society?

Not so, says Pinker, morality arises from a human need and is established in the Golden Rule, "Do unto others as you would like others to do unto you." From the beginning of time, in all ancient civilizations with their pantheons of capricious deities, long before Judaism, Christianity and Islam ever existed, this precept was the basis upon which human society flourished.

The concept of God came into being only because men were confused by forces of nature beyond their control and understanding, and needed to have an Almighty God to attribute these forces to. Eventually this God assumed responsibility for our code of morals as well.

Morality then became part of Religion, and consisted in obeying the dictates of God, and enforced by reward and punishment in this world and the next after-life. This "add-on" becomes necessary because in this world, no moral guardian can possibly detect and punish every wrong-doing, so we have to invent a God who, like Santa Claus, is always there – "he sees you when you're sleeping, he sees you when you're awake, he knows if you've been bad or good, so be good for goodness' sake." Otherwise, God will smite you down and damn you to hell and eternal fire.

This theistic morality, according to Pinker, has two basic flaws: (1) there is no good reason to believe that God exists, and (2) there is most certainly no God to dictate and enforce moral precepts.

First, there is no God because Science and Reason cannot prove that he exists, and because the reasons given for his existence – faith, revelation, scripture, tradition – cannot be trusted to explain why different religions declare mutually incompatible beliefs on how the human race was created, on how their devotees are to behave.

Scientific absurdities like Genesis have been refuted by Edwin Hubble with the Big Bang Theory; the story of Adam and Eve has been refuted by Darwin's Origin of the Species.

Second, there is no God to dictate and enforce, as Sextus Empericus in ancient times posited: "Is God willing to prevent evil, but not able? Then he isn't omnipotent. Is he able, but not willing? Then he is malevolent. Is he both able and willing? Then why doesn't he abolish evil?" David Hume puts it another way: Either God is not benevolent or he is not omnipotent; either way and in both ways, he is incapable of being God.

On the other hand, a few years ago, I wrote that there are 6 arguments used to prove there is a God: (1) Ontological (God exists because nothing greater than God can be conceived); (2) Cosmological (Everything has a cause except God who is the First Cause); (3) Argument of Miracles (Miracles happen, and only God can make it happen); (4) Argument from Religious Experience (Personal visions are direct encounters with God), (5) Argument of Utility (Belief in God is a great and indispensable moral influence), but the one argument with the widest appeal is (6) Teleological, or Argument of Grand Design, as I wrote it then, as follows:

Prior to the 20th century, most scientists believed that our universe never had a beginning, that mass, space, time and energy had always existed. Then in 1928 Edwin Hubble discovered that the universe is expanding, and using and reversing its velocity and direction, scientists calculated that the universe was born 13.8 billion years ago, from one explosion called the Big Bang, at a single time from a single pinpoint, from nothing, just like it says in the Bible, Genesis 1:1. The scientists have struggled so long up the mountain of knowledge, only to find that Bible scholars were already there at the top, long before they arrived.

If the rate of expansion of the Big Bang were a fraction less, the universe would have re-collapsed even before it reached its present size; if it were a fraction more, stars and galaxies could not have been formed, and we wouldn't be here. Conditions for life to exist (the existence and distribution of elements; the size, temperature, relative proximity of stars and planets) need to be just right that the chance against it to happen from a chance explosion of the Big Bang, defies the laws of probability – calculated to be one chance against a trillion repeated 12 times, or 10 to the 144th power, or 1 followed by 144 zeroes -- equivalent to the chance of a blind person finding one specific grain of sand from all the beaches in the world, or one person winning a mega-dollar lotto, a thousand consecutive times, with the same set of numbers. The only logical conclusion is that life came into being by deliberate design of a Superior Intellect, like the Bible says.

In 1953 Watson and Crick discovered the DNA in every cell of every living thing, a mere pinhead, each of which contains information equivalent to a stack of paperback books that would encircle the earth 5,000 times – an extremely complex software that reveals such intelligence that it staggers the imagination. Can it be that Science finally discovered God?

Now I remember, when I was in 4th year high school in Ateneo de Manila, being told that the first thing we do to understand the universe, the world we live in and man's role in it, is to understand the concept of entropy or disorder. In Physics it is expressed in the Second Law of Thermodynamics, which is that "in an isolated system, entropy never decreases." Confused? So was I! I asked my physics professor please to define entropy in terms I can understand, and he answered, after few unsuccessful attempts, "Well, a cup of coffee cools down, ice melts, fire warms you up, damn it, I cannot do better than that. My own professor in the University of the Philippines, could not make me understand, so forget the definition. Entropy is all around us, that is all I can say!" I was 14 years old then.

I was 20 years old in Boston, when I asked my professor in the Massachusetts Institute of Technology the same question, and he answered, "That question, Henares, is equivalent to asking me if I read Shakespeare, and my answer is that I read Shakespeare, but I cannot quote all of what he wrote." This is what Steven Pinter does in his new book "Enlightenment Now" devoting parts of several chapters to entropy, too long and too obtuse, and perhaps too erudite, to make sense to an old fogy, an engineer like me, who wants to explain a scientific law in a few paragraphs, or in one mathematical equation, like F=ma, or E=mc squared.

The dictionary does not help either. It defines Entropy as "a theoretical value measuring a property of a substance, as steam, under given conditions, upon which depends the amount of heat energy not transferable to mechanical work."

Today at the age of 94, with an IQ of 170, after having read 25,500 books in my lifetime, all of a sudden, this minute, this second, in a flash of divine inspiration, I woke up from a dreamless sleep, opened my eyes and at last, I begin to understand. So let me share my thoughts with you.

Entropy is a state of disorder, a state of being "disorderly and useless." Nature strives for disorder and uselessness, because the laws of probability dictate that there are infinitely more ways of being disorderly and useless, than being orderly and useful. It takes an artist an hour to build a sand castle, but it takes only a wave, the wind, a sea gull, and a small child to destroy it in seconds. It takes a jackass a minute to kick a barn down, an accidental fire to destroy it, or a tornado, an earthquake, a typhoon, a stick of dynamite and a hundred ways to blow it away in a few minutes --- but it takes a carpenter a whole week to build it.

13.8 billion years ago, in a split second, an incredibly dense atom exploded in a Big Bang. Suddenly, there was zero entropy, all was a flash of energy so useful and orderly that it gave birth to our Universe. Entropy increases as this incredible energy is wasted in moving galaxies away from each other. While stars are born, burn out and die, while black holes proliferate and suck into nothingness all matter within reach – entropy increases, till at last at the end of time and existence, the cold stars and dead planets are dispersed sparsely into the universe, a thin soup like salt in the ocean, useless and disorderly.

In my dissertation on the existence of God, I was wrong to assume that the universe is in a state of perpetual balance, and that this state is the result of a Grand Design of a superior intellect that we can do no better than to call God.

That instance of improbability measuring one chance against "one followed by 144 zeroes," is precisely the infinitely small sliver of a chance that life could exist in only one planet among 12 planets in our solar system, among a billion stars in our galaxy, among a hundred billion galaxies in the universe. The Second Law of Thermodynamics is at work against a vast and irresistible tide of entropy, the First Law of existence, expressed also in Murphy's Law (what <u>can</u> go wrong, <u>will</u> go wrong); Forest Gump's "Shit Happens"; Things fall apart; Rust never sleeps. Thus the Law of Entropy allow for only a hopeless past and a depressing future. Yet we stand in awe and in wonder of it all! ---

Because from one vantage point The Law of Entropy defines the fate of the universe and the ultimate purpose of life, mind and human striving – and that is, to use an infinitely small part of that energy -- to plant a tree, to sire a son, to write a book, to employ our knowledge and reasoning to the hundred million things that we do to build our civilizations, and to achieve our final destiny.

Because, according to the same Law of Entropy, randomly and unexpectedly, after 13.8 billion long long years, atoms arrange themselves to carve out infinitely minute oases of beneficial order and usefulness, to give us sunsets, rainbows, clouds, snowflakes, a stolen kiss, an orgasm, flora, fauna, the very existence of Man, and the most inspiring concept of God!

Let me answer the question posed: Is God necessary? I may for the sake of argument, concede that it is irrelevant whether or not we believe in the existence of God. But I do believe that whether he exists or not, God is necessary. If one did not believe that there is just and merciful God, and that immortal souls will meet again after death, life on earth would be intolerable. It would have no purpose, no everlasting love, no ultimate justice. Life would not be worth living. But we do believe, and hope and pray that someday in God's own time, we will be reunited with our beloved ones departed, my father, mother, many friends, and my ever loving wife Cecilia. It is this hope of reunion for all eternity that sustains us in our hour of loss and bereavement.

Again consider Blaise Pascal's Wager which states that to believe in God is the more rational choice, because if God really exists, we have eternal salvation to gain; but if God does not exist, we have nothing to gain or lose!

And still again, consider how I, at the age of 94, every ten minutes, as I feel the onset of a fart, truly and sincerely pray, "Please God, let it be gaseous, and not liquid or solid!"

Chapter 9.
Is the Human Race necessary?

In a previous article I ask if God is necessary, and quoted Steven Pinker who said that God does not exist, nor is he necessary. And he goes on to say that all that is necessary is Reason, Science and Humanism, and the revitalization of all the human values derived from Age of Enlightenment that originated from the Western World: Life and the Pursuit of Happiness; Liberty, Equality, Fraternity; Democracy, Free Will, Free Market Economy, Individualism, Self Determination, Liberalism.

And counter to the Enlightenment are obviously (1) Religious Faith and (2) the Tribalism of clans, tribes, ethnic groups, religion, race, class and nation-states. It seems that Steven Pinker is afflicted with that demonic of all idolatries -- arrogant Self-Worship, of the white race and the Western Man -- that leads ultimately to self-destruction, which we will prove later. It is our honest opinion that Pinker is indulging in intellectual masturbation.

Endless are the ways that man worships, ranging from the horrible to the sublime to the ridiculous -- proof that whatever else he may be, Man is a religious being -- the only creature, according anthropologist William Howells, "who comprehends things he cannot see and believes in things he cannot comprehend."

Most living religions assume that they come directly from the hand of God, unique like the biblical Melchisedec, "without father, without mother, without descent, having neither beginning of days, nor end of life." But that is not so. The Dead Sea Scrolls show that some ideas and rites of the New Testament are similar to those of the Qumran sect that existed a century before Christ. The 4,000-year-old Babylonian epic of Gilgamesh finds striking parallels in the Genesis story of Noah's ark.

And how can faiths which hold salvation to be a reward of man's own striving, merge with faiths that insist salvation is an unmerited gift of God? Is truth found at the end of a human quest, or is truth revealed by an act of Revelation? How to synthesize the Christian conviction that Divine Revelation culminated with Jesus, with the Muslim conviction that a more complete revelation came with Mohammed, and the Jewish belief that neither surpassed the Law and the Prophets?

Many non-believers like Pinker, turn to the philosophy of Humanism which holds the view that men have but one life to lead and should make the most of it in terms of creative work and happiness, but that is also a faith, faith in Homo Deus. Communism which regards religion as the opium of the people, is fast developing into a church. If as the New Testament says, faith is "the substance of things hoped for, the evidence of things unseen," then Communism, with its promise of a classless social order and equal sharing of all men in the benefits of life, surely is a faith.

It may be that God is imbedded in the human DNA. In their religions, men do not really differ. They seek the favor of their gods, protection from danger, community with their fellows, courage in the hour of conflict, comfort in the hour of grief, guidance in their daily concerns, and some hope for immortality.

Today the march of science makes it imperative that Man be saved from that most demonic of all idolatries -- arrogant Self-Worship that leads ultimately to self-destruction.

Salvation comes only when, in the words of the prophet Micah, our faith inspires us "to do justly, to love mercy, and to walk humbly with God."

It is evident that Steven Pinker is trying to elevate Western Civilization and the white man, who caused so much tears and suffering to the colored races with his notions of racial superiority, to the level where we may ignore the historical grievances that have to be redressed before we proceed to pursue our Final Destiny.

Equality is unachievable. We need only to observe that handsome men tend to marry beautiful women, and that the rich and the powerful also tend to marry rich and powerful mates, and the good-looking ones too. In the long run, the human race will continue to be separated into two groups, (1) the few rich, powerful and good-looking, and (2) the many poor, powerless and ugly. And not humans, but non-human fictitious persons with the human right to enter into contracts and own property, Nations and Corporations, rule the earth and own most of its resources.

Comes now Yuval Noah Harari, a Hebrew, of a race considered inferior by the Germanic races, which includes the Germans, the Dutch, the English, and the American WASPs (White Anglo-Saxon Protestant), in his book, Homo Deus, contradicting everything that Steven Pinker wrote about the Final Destiny of the Human Race.

Recent scientific discoveries, Harari writes, undermine the liberal philosophy of the Enlightenment. Liberals uphold free markets and democratic elections because they believe every human being is a uniquely valuable individual, whose free choices are the ultimate sources of authority. This belief is obsolete, and Steven Pinter is wrong, because:

First, Liberalism succeeded because in the past, political, economic, and military sense combined to ascribe value to every human being; in democratic elections because of his vote, in the Industrial Revolution because he runs the machines, in the army if he capable of firing a shot. In the future, however, robots take over the industrial machines, sophisticated smart weapons need only a finger to push a button to conduct a war (mutually assured destruction, MAD, makes world wars unlikely) and algorithms imbedded in net-working systems take over control over the conduct of human affairs. The need for and the value of individual human beings are considerably diminished. We will all have been devalued, hahaha, like Iraqis and Afghans. Perhaps Human Beings are no longer necessary.

Second, the system will continue to find value in humans collectively in the mass (the objective is still to keep them happy and prosperous), but not in unique individuals separately.

Third, the system will continue to find value in a few unique individuals, but these will constitute a new elite of upgraded super-humans above the mass of the population.

In such a world, there is really no such thing as Free Will or Free Choice. Over the last century, bio-scientists discovered that there is neither soul, nor free will nor self – but only genes, hormones and neurons that obey the same physical and chemical laws governing the rest of reality. With state regulation, there is no real Free Markets, with monopoly by large corporations, bolstered by patents, trademarks, price-fixing, cartels, combinations and conspiracies in restraint of trade.

Actually forces are already at work in this Information Age, that tremendously increase the amount of goods available at little marginal cost, "free stuff" that are slowly undermining the Capitalistic System itself. E-mail is free, the Post Office has lost its relevance. Education is free for those who can surf the Internet.

Wikipedia with its 27,000 volunteers sharing information, had driven encyclopedias out of business.

Books are so cheap, easily replicated at the touch of the button, that libraries are no longer viable. The dissemination of news is free, newspapers are on the verge of extinction. Almost all the people in this planet own cellphones; that means that everybody enjoys connectivity, and land-lines and phone companies will eventually be extinct. The digital camera was invented, and Kodak was forced into bankruptcy; now everybody owns a camera, taking perfect pictures without limit without using a single sliver of silver which used to be a component of the photographic film. With the invention of the computer, writing books and putting them in the hands of readers, is available to anyone who wants to do it. I read one book a day for 70 years of my 94 years of age, I have lived the lives and absorbed the thoughts of the authors of the 25,500 books I read, yet everything I know is available to morons at the flick of the button in the Internet. These are just a few of the many "free stuff" that are changing our lives, as the result of the convergence of digital technologies in the smart phone, the other free stuff that come with cellphones: clocks, maps, calendars, cameras, long playing records, tape recorders, cassette recorders, compact discs, books and magazines, even department stores.

And the miracle of it is that this Information Age is undermining the ability of the Capitalistic system itself to contrive Scarcity out of Abundance in order to generate profits. The very concept of property, patent and trademark protection is being challenged. Netizens can download practically any movie that has ever been filmed and practically every song ever composed without having to pay the people who produced them. Corporate secrets are repeatedly being hacked and leaked to the public. I believe the Capitalistic System will eventually fade away, eventually into some form of Christian Socialism that existed for centuries, in such Catholic religious orders as the Benedictines and Augustinians. The economics of caring and sharing is at hand. The Age of Information is already preparing the world for Project Zero – because its aims are zero carbon energy system, the production of machines, products and services with zero marginal costs, and the reduction of necessary labor time as close as possible to zero.

In the Information Age of unlimited Abundance, the end purpose is to pay every one of working age, an unconditional basic income from the state, enough to guarantee freedom from want, all the things he needs to live a decent life even if he does not work. It allows everyone to volunteer, set up co-ops, edit Wikipedia, learn how to use 3D design software, or just exist; to space out periods of work, make a late entry or early exit from working life, switch easily in and out of stressful jobs. We will be a classless society of consumers who are also producers, designers, artists and lovers.

As Harari expresses it, the main products of the 21st century will not be textiles, vehicles and weapons, but bodies to a state of health, and brains and minds to a higher IQ and EQ. While the Industrial Revolution created the Working Class, the Information Age will create a Class of Useless and Pampered Masses, with a guaranteed high standard of living by robots, drones and net-worked algorithms. Democracy and free market will both collapse, once Google and Facebook know us better than we know ourselves, and authority will shift from individual humans to net-worked algorithms. Humans will not fight machines but will merge with them when Artificial Intelligence surpasses human intelligence. Contrary to Sci-fi movies, we are heading towards marriage, not war.

This is the shape of the new world, and the gap between those who get on board and those left behind will be larger than the gap between industrial empires and agrarian tribes, larger even than the gap between Homo Sapiens and the Neanderthals. The way humans have treated animals is a good indicator of how upgraded humans will treat the pampered useless masses.

This is the next stage of Evolution. This is Homo Deus, the Human God. So, are ordinary, run-of-the-mill, garden-variety human beings no longer necessary? Devaluated into useless masses that exist only to be pampered and tolerated?

Chapter 10.
The Original Sin

In 1966, in his third year high in La Salle Greenhills, my son Atom (A for Alfredo, Tom for Tomas, Atom Bum we called him), favorite protégé of Ninoy Aquino, decided with my help to make a movie as a substitute for a term paper, entitled "The Original Sin" the story of Mankind from Adam and Eve to the last two people on earth -- adroitly pacing the film from a farce (Genesis), to a serious documentary decrying pollution and the rape of Mother Earth, to a fantasy (the Doctrine of Divine Recall), and a human drama (Atom and Martita) with an O. Henry ending. The script is as follows:

In the beginning God created the heavens and the earth and everything else, and saw that they were perfect.

Then almost as an afterthought, God created Adam and Eve, and that's when the trouble began. He forbade them to partake of the Apple of His eye, the fruit of the knowledge of good and evil. But a snake in the grass enticed Eve to taste the Apple, and to get Adam to do the same. When Adam was all fired up to do what comes naturally, Eve demurred, "Close your eyes and open your lips, darling, and I'll give you a big big kiss." When he did, Eve shoved the Apple into his mouth. God was mad and ordered Adam and Eve exiled.

They went forth and multiplied.

And so the human race began. But oh such a bad beginning!

The human race began, and what a rat race!

Man multiplied so fast that he soon covered the face of the earth. Human beings scoured the ground they walked on; poisoned the air they breathed with fumes from their cars and factories. Indiscriminate use of insecticides eliminated the insects, and the birds that fed on the insects, and the plants that needed to be pollenized, till eventually came the Silent Spring --- no birds, no crickets, no plants, no flowers. They poisoned the seas and rivers with industrial waste. Chemical detergents proved indestructible by the scavengers of nature, and soon permanently contaminated the waters of the earth.

And now having raped poor Mother Earth, the human species reached out into space to ravage the rest of the Universe!

"Man has destroyed the balance of Nature and the Grand Harmony of the Universe," said Father Jake Bern (named after

Of Time and Space, Of God and Man

Joaquin Bernas, the only Jesuit in the good graces of Opus Dei), as he expounded on his Doctrine of Divine Recall in the year 2000 AD. Preaching before a small fanatic group of true believers, he proposed the final self-destruction of the human race.

"The Existence of Man is a false note in the Grand Harmony of the Universe. Man is destined for God's Kingdom in Heaven; his Earthly Existence was a mistake of Nature, an evolutionary accident that has destroyed the Balance of Nature.

"Balance, Order, and Harmony can only be restored when Man wipes himself completely from the face of the earth. God wants to recall Man from his earthly existence. Man must make the Supreme Sacrifice and get his reward in Heaven. All must come, and Now!"

And with that statement, Father Jake Bern put a pistol into his mouth and blew his own brains out.

Fifty years later in 2050 AD, the Doctrine of Divine Recall became the world religion. People began to kill themselves with hallucinatory drugs, and death became a beautiful religious experience. By 2075 AD, the World Government decreed that all women must henceforth practice birth control. Thus in that fateful year was born the last generation of the human race.

Twenty years later in 2095 AD, the babies grew old enough to understand and appreciate the Doctrine of Divine Recall. And in an unprecedented exercise of sovereign power, all the people on earth opted for the Final Solution --- the systematic self-extermination of the human race.

The mass suicide was carried out chronologically from the eldest to the youngest, till at last, the last generation of human beings --- the generation of 2075 AD --- took its turn on the rack of self-destruction. This was to be the Final Act of the Last Exodus, the glorious finale to the Fall of Man.

Bernadette was an ugly woman, a frigid misanthrope, and a fanatic true believer in the Doctrine of Divine Recall. She was chosen to be the last person on earth, entrusted with the awesome duty to oversee the death of the last batch, and kill herself.

But there were two from the last batch who plotted blasphemy. They were in love, and wanted to remain alive to produce a new human race. Their names were Atom and Martita.

Bernadette discovered, after the suicide of the last batch, that Atom and Martita had disappeared. Using a sensitive detector computer, Bernadette found them making love in a bed of wild flowers, amidst a sunset that bathed the scene with kaleidoscopic colors as far as the eyes can see, beside yawning abysmic chasms and thunderous cataracts that stagger the mind into thoughts of Time, Space, Eternity and God. This must have been how the earth looked in the beginning --- pure, pristine, virginal --- before Man came into existence.

Bernadette fired a shot into the face of Martita, and as she shuddered her final gasp, Bernadette stood there, triumphant, her pistol pointed at the last man on earth --- Atom.

Atom waited for the instant of doom. It came with a deafening roar, and momentarily stunned him Atom looked up to see the last woman on earth, smiling, her one hand stretched out with an offering of peace --- a ripe red apple. With the other hand, she discarded her pistol, and began to unbutton her dress.

And so the human race started again. But oh, another bad beginning!

The End.

Chapter 11.
The Story of Man

The proper study of mankind is Man, said Alexander Pope. Tell me the story of mankind, begged my young daughter Juno, then a sweet young lady with all the curious wisdom of her six years of age. Who can resist the challenge of one on whom the future of mankind depends? So I answered, sit still, my child, I said, and listen to this human drama, the denouement of which may yet be in your hands.

Once upon a time, thousands and thousands of years ago, a strange curious-minded creature stared through matted hair at the brilliant pin-points of light set in the velvety blackness of the night.

He asked himself "Why?" And with that question he drifted away from the beasts of the field and unconsciously started on the road to destiny.

It was a road beset by perils and pitfalls that this bewildered creature took -- this half human creature struggling to be a Man.

He was weak, but he was not helpless. His skin was bared to the elements, but he tamed fire to give him warmth and comfort. His was not the agility of the tiger nor the strength of the elephant, but he chipped the sides of a stone to fashion a weapon that gave him mastery over the animal world.

He viewed the fishes roving the deep and found that by gouging out a log into a crude canoe, he too could roam the seas. He watched birds rise in the air and wondered if he too could ever fly.

Man's progress was slow, and the sun did not always shine on his path.

Once, amidst the terror-laden blackness of the night, he stopped and realized he was terribly alone. There, in his loneliness, he found a Friend. For out of the night came a voice saying, "I am the Lord thy God..."

In a vision of another world, Man saw things more beautiful than he ever saw before. He saw pearly gates and golden streets and jeweled palaces. In seeing, he found peace and contentment and a promise of things to come.

When the vision faded, Man was filled with envious yearning. He could not wait for another world. He wanted his heaven here on earth. He would build it himself, aye, and be like... God!

Eagerly, passionately, he set himself upon his task. He took the green of the pastures, the gold of the hills, the might of the rivers, fashioned them with his hands, his heart, his mind -- and transformed them into power. He built ships that plowed the heaving oceans, planes that swept the virgin heights.

He bored tunnels through insurmountable barriers of rock. He moved mountains. He sent his merest whisper echoing throughout the world. He conquered time and space, he conquered his whole planet...

But he could not conquer himself. Evil crept into his soul and manifested itself in wars, cruelty and bloodshed. He sought peace but he brought only turmoil and confusion unto himself.

A strange restlessness grew within him. The light of knowledge served only to extend the circumference of the surrounding darkness. The more he learned, the more he realized how ignorant, how insignificant he really was, and how utterly unworthy he was of the heaven he was to build.

He who wished to be God found out that he was just a small, crawling mass of impure carbohydrate, marooned in a bit of stardust adrift in the vastness of the infinite.

Then suddenly Man made three tremendous discoveries.

First, in an infinitely minute particle of matter, he found the source of power of suns and stars.

Second, he discovered the means to free himself from the embrace of Mother Earth and reach out into the timeless space beyond.

But more exciting than nuclear power and the race to the stars, is the coming Biological Revolution. In the coiled structure of the DNA molecule and the complex arrangements of its atoms lie the final secrets of life and heredity. Once he masters its genetic code, man's powers will truly be godlike, with the ability to shape his own evolution, and create new forms of humanity.

The mystery of all creation awaits his coming.

Awestruck and confused, Man stands at the threshold of a new era. The key is in his hand. Hopeful, yet afraid, he hesitates at the door before him. What thoughts, what prayers, what visions take place within him!

Perhaps Man can now be a God. Perhaps he can now build his pearly gates and golden streets and jeweled palaces. Perhaps.

But in the light of his human failings, he wonders if he can trust himself with these awesome secrets. Perhaps, he was never meant to be a God. Perhaps the revelation of these secrets will destroy Man, will blast the world back into its elements...

...and perhaps, millions and millions of years will pass before there is a new world and a new planet... and another curious-minded creature, staring through matted hair at the brilliant pin-points of light set in the velvety blackness of the night.

Chapter 12.
Scientific Atheistic Humanism

Religion is a Big Deal. The Search for Truth, in contrast, is a journey that starts from age-old questions that have always bothered us since the beginning of time: Who am I? What is the purpose of my existence? What is right, what is wrong, what is good, what is evil? This journey leads us through unexplored byways to undetermined destinations, sometimes to the discovery of a Great Truth, sometimes back to Religion in a Buddhist monastery on top of the Himalayas.

On the other hand, Religion provides us with all the answers to our questions: You are in this world, to serve God, to love him, and to be with him forever after death. Here is the deal: our priests will tell you what is right, wrong, good and evil – that masturbation, birth control, and missing Sunday mass are bad – and you must obey us or suffer eternal damnation.

The Search for Truth is originally the domain of Science and Reason. Isaac Newton is a religious person, but he discovered Gravitation and Calculus. Thomas Jefferson was also religious, but he authored "self-evident Truths." The march of Science and Reason has led to the discovery of Great Truths, Evolution of Darwin, Faraday's electric motor, Einstein's Relativity – but it also led to the greatest religion of all, Humanism, the self-worship of Man as Homo Deus.

As a Religion, Humanism is a Big Deal too. You have only one life to live and we will help you make the best of it. Belief in Science, Reason and your Fellow Man will eventually liberate you from hunger, epidemics and violence, to unprecedented levels of prosperity, health and harmony, according to Aldous Huxley and Steven Pinker (author of "Enlightenment Now").

Yuval Noah Harari, author of "Homo Deus" argues further that there are actually three sects of Humanism: **Liberal** Humanism whose main goal is **Liberty**; **Social** Humanism whose main goal is **Equality**; and **Evolutionary** Humanism whose main goal is the **Survival of the Fittest**. Like other religions, it led to violence in a grand scale, to two World Wars and one bloody Cold War.

In World War I, Liberal Humanism of the USA and Western democracies, clashed Germany's Evolutionary Humanism which promoted Nietzsche's Superman. Germany shipped Marxist Vladimir

Lenin into Russia to promote Social Humanism which seeks to establish a classless society where Equality dictates that "to each according to his need, and from each according to his talent," like the Christian Socialism of the Benedictines and Jesuits. In this war, the main casualty was the Divine Right of Kings. But Humanism survived in the democracies of the West, in the Communism of Russia, and the Fascism of Italy and Nazism of Hitler's Germany.

World War II pitted the Liberal Humanism of the Western Democracies against the Evolutionary Humanism of Axis powers (Italy, Germany and Japan). The Social Humanism of Russian Communism entered the fray on the side of the Western democracies, suffered the most casualties, and proved to be the decisive factor in the victory against Hitler's German *Herrenvolk.*

That left the Cold War of the Liberal Humanism of the West against Social Humanism of the Soviet Union, which was carried on by surrogates on both sides, mostly by military dictatorships like Chile's Pinochet, the Shah of Iran, Argentina's Peron, the Philippines' Marcos, Batista, Duvalier, Vietnam's Ngo Diem, China's Chiang Kai-chek, Rumania's Ceausescu, North Korea's Kim – all tinhorn imitations of Adolf Hitler, the ultimate symbol of Evolutionary Humanism.

This ended in 1991 with the collapse of the Soviet Union and East European Communism. But Chinese Communism with its concessions to free markets and private initiative, survived and prospered to carry on the Socialist Dream.

An American of 1914 suddenly transported a hundred years to 2018, would think that the world hardly changed, with the triumphant Liberal Humanism in ascendancy, unaware that in the intervening years, 37 million died in World War I, 85 million in World War II, 88 million in the Cold War, a total of 210 million in only one century. Christians caused 700 million deaths in 20 centuries, an average of only 35 million dead per century. This makes Scientific Atheistic Humanism the deadliest religion ever.

Chapter 13.
Narrative of Human Progress

Entro, Evo, Info. According to cognitive scientist Steven Pinker -- Entropy, Evolution, Information are three concepts that define the narrative of human progress, our tragic beginnings and the means we employ to improve our existence.

The first keystone in understanding the human condition is the concept of Entropy or disorder and uselessness, as defined in the Second Law of Thermodynamics, which states that in an isolated system (one that does not interact with its environment) entropy never decreases. The First Law is about the conservation of energy; the Third Law is that the temperature of absolute zero (minus 273.15 degrees Centigrade on the Celsius scale) is unattainable. Don't chew on that if you flunked high school Physics.

I explained in detail how Entropy works in Chapter 8 of this book (Is God Necessary?), no need to repeat it. It is enough to explain that Entropy is a state of disorder, a state of being "disorderly and useless." Nature strives for disorder and uselessness, because the laws of probability dictate that there are infinitely more ways of being disorderly and useless, than being orderly and useful. It takes an artist an hour to build a sand castle, but it takes only a wave, the wind, a sea gull, and a small child to destroy it in seconds. The Law of Entropy defines the fate of the universe and the ultimate purpose of life, mind and human striving – and that is, to use an infinitely small part of the energy being grossly dissipated in the universe -- to plant a tree, to sire a son, to write a book, to employ our knowledge and reasoning to the hundred million things that we do to build our civilizations, and to achieve our final destiny.

The second keystone in understanding the human condition is the concept of Evolution, defined as "the process by which different kinds of living organisms are thought to have developed and diversified from earlier forms during the history of the earth" as conceptualized by Charles Darwin. According to Pinker, there is no God, no Supreme Being to create the universe by Intelligent Design. There is only the random and unexpected development for long long periods of time, by the process of Natural Selection of species, to achieve the Survival of the Fittest, that is, to keep them alive to absorb energy against the irresistible tide of entropy.

The third keystone in understanding the human condition is the concept of Information, that is, the processing of Information -- the development of a unique language that lent itself to gossiping, and telling stories about things that do not exist – the appearance of a new ways of thinking and communicating that constitutes the Cognitive Revolution.

Social cooperation is our key to survival and reproduction. It is not enough for individual men and women to know the whereabouts of predators like lions and preys like deer. It is more important for them to know who in their tribe hates whom, who is sleeping with whom, who is honest, who is a cheat – reliable information about who could be trusted, meant that small bands could expand into larger bands, that humans could develop tighter and more sophisticated types of cooperation. But the most unique part of the language of the Homo Sapiens is his ability to transmit information about things that do not exist at all, about entities that he has never seen, touched or smelled. Legends, myths, gods and religions appeared for the first time during the Cognitive Revolution. Telling stories of fiction allowed us not merely to imagining things, but also to do it and believe it collectively. We can weave common myths like the biblical creation story, nationalist myths of modern states like (hahaha) American Exceptionalism, and legal fiction of the existence of corporations, money and financial instruments – such myths allow Sapiens to cooperate flexibly in large numbers.

Ants and bees cooperate too in large numbers, but they do so rigidly and only with close relatives. Wolves and chimpanzees cooperate far more flexibly than ants, but they do so only with small numbers of individuals that they know intimately. Sapiens can cooperate in extremely flexible ways with countless numbers of strangers. That is why we Sapiens rule the world, while ants eat our leftovers, and chimps are locked up in zoos and research laboratories.

Now to the narrative of human progress, that came with the Age of Enlightenment, when Reason and Science came to release us from age-old Ignorance. What is Progress? One might think the question is so subjective and relative that it is forever unanswerable, but Pinker writes, actually it is very easy to answer.

Most people agree that life is better than death. Health is better than sickness. Sustenance is better than hunger. Abundance is better than poverty. Peace is better than war. Safety is better than danger. Freedom is better than tyranny. Equal rights are better than bigotry and discrimination. Literacy is better than illiteracy. Knowledge is better than ignorance. Intelligence is better than dull-wittedness. Happiness is better than misery. Opportunities to enjoy family, friends, culture and nature are better than drudgery and monotony. All these things can be measured. If they have increased over time, that is progress.

Life. The struggle to stay alive is the primal urge of all animate beings, and human beings deploy their ingenuity and conscious resolve to stave off death as long a possible. The eternal quest to find the Fountain of Youth attests to that. The life expectancy for hunter-gathers was 32.5 years of age. The Agricultural revolution increased the population but drastically reduced the life-expectancy due to infectious diseases that infested crowded towns and cities, the starchy diet, wars and famine. In the mid-18th century, the life expectancy for the world was 29 years of age. In Europe and America at that time it was around 35 years of age, and it was parked there for the previous 225 years for which we have data. The death of a child affects the average life expectancy much more than the death of an adult, because it brings a zero to the equation. Then a miracle happened in the 19th century, when child mortality plunged a hundredfold to a fraction of a percentage point in developed countries and the plunge went global. In 2015, the life expectancy for the whole world is 71.4 years. That is progress. The best projection of our multi-century war on death is Stein's Law – "Things that can't go forever, don't" – as amended by Davies's Corollary – "Things that can't go on forever, can go on much longer than you think."

Health. For most of human history, the strongest force of death was infectious disease, the nasty feature of evolution in which small, rapidly reproducing organisms make their living at our expense, and hitch a ride from body to body, in bugs, worms and bodily effluvia. Epidemics killed by the millions, wiping out whole civilizations, and visiting sudden misery on local populations – bubonic plague, yellow fever, cholera, smallpox, influenza, malaria, typhoid, tuberculosis, dysentery, polio, syphilis, AIDS. But the ever-creative Homo Sapiens fought back with quackery such as prayer, sacrifice, bloodletting, toxic metals, homeopathy, and squeezing a hen to death against an infected body part. But in the late 18th century, with the invention of vaccination, and accelerating in the 19th with the acceptance of the germ theory of disease, the tide of battle began to turn. Hand-washing, midwifery, mosquito control, and especially the protection of drinking water by public sewerage and chlorination, sterilization by boiling water, antiseptics and antibiotics would come to save billions and billions of lives. Anyone who forgets Edward Jenner, Louis Pasteur, Joseph Lister, Frederick Banting, Charles Best, William Osler, Alexander Fleming, or Jonas Salk, should be consigned to the ninth circle of hell for sheer ingratitude!

Sustenance. Another mean trick played on us by evolution and entropy is our ceaseless need for energy, that is, food to give us that energy. Famine has long been part of the human condition. The Bible speaks of the seven long years of drought in ancient Egypt; India and China had always been vulnerable to famine, because millions of people subsisted on rice that was watered by erratic monsoon rains or fragile irrigation systems, subject to infestation of locusts and rats, and had to be transported across great distances to people who need them. Historians chronicle contemporary first-hand accounts of famines – starving children begging for crumbs of bread to still the pangs of hunger, eyes sunk deep in the head, lips pale and covered with slime, the skin hard with the bones showing through, the belly nothing but a pouch hanging down empty – desperate peasants eating grass or human flesh, drawing on the entrails of the dead to fill their own bellies, children sold by parents, collective suicides. In 1798 Thomas Malthus explained that famines are unavoidable because population increases geometrically (1,2,4,8,16,32,64) while food production increases arithmetically (1,2,3,4,5,6). Yet miracle of miracles, in recent times, despite burgeoning populations, the underdeveloped world is actually feeding itself – even China where 1.3 billion people consume 3,100 calories per person per day, equivalent to what is needed by a highly active young man – even India where 1 billion consume 2,400 calories per person per day, what is needed by a highly active middle-aged man – even the whole of Africa every person consumes 2,600 calories per day, even more than Indians do. Where did Malthus's math go wrong? For one thing, population growth need not increase in geometrical ratio indefinitely, because as people grow richer and more babies survive, they also tend to have fewer babies. For another, food supply can grow, not arithmetically, but geometrically when knowledge of science is applied to selective breeding, genetic engineering, crop rotation, use of tractors and fertilizers, and network of roads and railroads to bring the farm produce to the market before it rots (as every farmer and gardener knows). For the first time in history, the third millennium witnessed that more people died from eating too much than died from eating too little.

Wealth. In a world controlled by Entropy and Evolution, streets are not paved with gold, nor sidewalks with pastries, and cooked fish do not land at our feet. During the Agriculture era, economics was a zero-sum game, per capita production and the size of the economic pie remained the same, so that the wealthy became wealthier by making the poor even poorer. That is why Jesus said that it is easier for a camel to go through the eye of a needle than a rich man's chance to enter heaven. He assumes that the rich extort their wealth from the poor. That is no longer true during the modern scientific era. For this we credit the greatest conqueror of history, a conqueror possessed of extreme tolerance and adaptability, thereby turning people into ardent disciples. This conqueror is Money, and its most ardent disciples are merchants, conquerors and prophets. For merchants the entire world was a single market, and all humans are potential customers. For conquerors, the entire world is a single kingdom and all humans are potential subjects. For prophets, the entire world holds a single truth and all humans are potential believers. All strive to create a "free market" economic order applicable to everyone everywhere; a universal religion that everyone will believe in; and an international order of governance based on a Social Contract between the government and the governed. But hopes and predictions don't make it true.

Steven Pinker is wrong when he assumes it is Western Capitalism that created the wealth of the world, or that the wealth of the world may be measured by currencies like the dollar whose worth is variable – unlike the kilometer that is a trusted measure of distance and the kilogram which is a reliable measure of weight. What creates wealth is something that is common to all nations, whether Capitalist or Communist, whether Democratic or Totalitarian – and that is Money and Credit.

The Central Bank systems around the world allows banks are allowed to lend as much as P10 for every P1 dollar of deposit, so that

90% of the money in bank accounts is not covered by actual coins and paper currency. Sounds like a fraudulent Ponzi scheme, but it is not. If all the depositors demand to have their money back, the bank will promptly collapse, and the depositor will lose their savings, but chances are, the government will save the bank by lending it the needed cash, and guaranteeing reimbursement to the depositors. This whole system is not a deception but a tribute to the amazing abilities of the human imagination. Assets are due not only to Net Worth, but also to loans in the form of Receivables which are really convertible to Assets in the future. What enables banks and the entire economy to survive and flourish is our Trust in the Future. This Trust is the sole backing of all the money in the world. Unlimited credit, money made out nothing, is made available to generate Economic Growth during the Scientific era. In the past, no such credit was available because bankers did not trust the future. There is a distinction between wealth and capital: wealth is for conspicuous consumption; capital is for investment in the Future. Wealth is for kings and nobles and festivities and fine clothes and unproductive things. Capital is for shopkeepers and bankers and board chairmen in inconspicuous suits, and machines and labor and raw materials and things that are productive for the benefit of the human race.

For the last 500 years, the idea of unlimited growth and progress, and ever larger economic pie took hold, credit ballooned into large, long-term, low-interest loans, exceeding current income. Unlimited power (wind, solar, nuclear, biogas), and the instruments of efficiency (fictitious entities with limited liability, specialization, division of labor, standardization of parts, time and motion studies) gave us prosperity beyond our wildest dreams!

Inequality. But is all this wealth going only to the richest one percent who skim off all the economic growth, while everyone else is treading water or slowly sinking?? It is a fact that in the United States, the share of income that goes to the richest 1 percent, grew from 8 percent in 1980 to 18 percent in 2015; and the share of the richest 0.10 percent, grew from 2 percent in 1980 to 8 percent in 2015. Steven Pinter glosses over this, and contends that in the Age of Enlightenment, Reason and Science, economics is not a zero-sum game; that the pie also gets much bigger so that while the richest may be richer still, the poor may also be richer, though not in the same proportion. He makes a credible thesis of this, citing inventions like cars and refrigerators, and innovations like the cellphone, Internet and the "free stuff" of the Information Age that make possible untold riches beyond the dreams of ordinary men. And for this he gives credit to Western Capitalism, and demeans the contribution of Marxist Communism. He is wrong.

Capitalism is a gladiator sport that gives the prize to the strongest, where inequality is the inevitable. Communism seeks to realize the Socialist dream of a classless society where "each serves according to his talents, and each receives according to his needs," exactly the same achieved by the Christian Socialism of religious orders like Benedictines, Augustinians, and Jesuits that endured for the last 2,000 years of the Christian era. Western Capitalism cruelly exploited its own labor class (read the novels of Charles Dickens), kidnapped and enslaved black men to serve a useless class of slave-owners, conquered colonies of "inferior races" by force of arms to secure a source of raw materials and a market for its manufactured products, exterminated indigenous aborigines of North America and Australia by deliberate genocide, and poisoned the Chinese wholesale with opium from India, ending an ancient civilization that coexisted with ancient Egypt and lasted for 4,000 years. Too cruel to endure, Western Capitalism survived because it adopted Socialist ideas like minimum wage, health care, welfare state, labor rights and safety nets for the poor and unemployed, and laws against the exploitation of women and children. Chinese Communism survived because it adopted Capitalistic ideas like Free Markets and Private Initiative, while keeping the means of production firmly in the hands of the state. Soviet Communism failed because its doddering old leaders never learned to adopt and adapt, while continuing a totalitarian regime that became intolerable. Capitalism is plagued with unsynchronized waves of supply and demand that causes business cycles of prosperity and depression, and contrives Scarcity out of Abundance to preserve profits of Corporate Monopoly, cartels, patents and copyrights, and other combinations and conspiracies in restraint of trade, that results in unavoidable waste by the "creative destruction" of inefficient competitors. Communism contrives to control the means of production to synchronize with the Needs (not necessarily the Wants of the populace), which has an "inelastic" demand that seldom varies, to avoid the plague of Business Cycles and waste of scarce but valuable resources; it is doubtful that poor nations late in development can achieve real industrialization and first class national power without Socialism or Communism.

The Environment. But is this Progress sustainable in the face of Climate Change?? Yes, answers Pinker, despite the Green Movement and the manifestos of Al Gore and Pope Francis, whom he chastises as a "quasi-religious ideology against corporate rapacity" that do not realize that "some degree of pollution is an inescapable consequence of the Second Law of Thermodynamics. When people use energy to a zone of structure in their bodies and homes, they must increase entropy elsewhere in the environment in the form of waste, pollution, and other forms of disorder." Looks like Steven Pinker is taking the side of President Donald Trump in rejecting the Paris Agreement on Climate Change as part of his America First policy, condemning "Greenism laced with misanthropy, an indifference to starvation, an indulgence for ghoulish fantasies of a depopulated planet...." Humans need to use energy to lift themselves out of poverty to which Entropy and Evolution consign them, he declares, and if that means burning coal and fossil fuels, then so be it, because Reason, Science and Capitalism will find the answer. They always did in the past, and they will do so in the future; and humanity is NOT on an irrevocable path to ecological suicide. There is only one flaw to this argument: Pinker assumes that the ruling class of Capitalists are reasonable men who use Science to benefit the human race. That is demonstrably untrue, American Capitalists are the most rapacious class on this planet, who have made Greed a creed of entitlement and impunity, who poisoned our air with lead in their gasoline, justifying it in the face of scientific evidence to the contrary; who burned coal and fossil fuels, and despoiled the seas with oil spills and plastic garbage in the same way; who made cow's milk which is an allergen, a substitute for breastmilk; who ravaged our economies with monopolistic practices, cartels and watered stock that necessitated the passage of the Sherman and Clayton Anti-Trust Acts, etcetera, etcetera; and do not really give a damn if the rise in sea levels would erase coastal cities and archipelagos. It is America First and everybody else second! It is my honest opinion that Donald Trump is a bullshit artist who does not know the difference between fact and fiction, and does not care to know, whose main supporters are rednecks and white trash with notions of racial superiority, religious nuts, hillbillies, gun-crazy goons, and Steven Pinker who indulges in intellectual masturbation.

Terrorism. In recent years highly publicized terrorist attacks and rampage killings have set the world on edge and fostered an illusion that we live in newly dangerous times. In 2016, a majority of Americans named terrorism as the most important issue facing the country, said that they are worried that they or a family member would be a victim, and identified ISIS as a threat to the existence or survival of the United States. But yes, all this is an illusion. Terrorism is a unique hazard because it combines a major dread with a minor harm. The Table on Deaths in 2014:

	USA	Western World	Europe
Terrorism	14	175	38,422
War	28	5	97,496
Homicide	15,696	3,962	437,000
Vehicle Accidents	35,398	19,219	1,250.000
All Accidents	136,053	126,482	5,000,000
All Deaths	2,626.418	3,877.598	56,400,000

Americans are 350 times as likely to be killed by homicide as in a terrorist attack; 800 times as likely to die in a car crash; 3,000 times as likely to die in an accident of any kind. In Western Europe, the relative danger of terrorism was higher than in the USA. Western Europeans are less murderous than Americans, with about a quarter of their homicide rate; only 20 times more likely to to die by homicide (which is already quite rare) than by a terrorist attack; 100 times more likely to die in a car crash; 700 times more likely to die in an accident of any kind. Though the USA and Europe contain about a tenth of the world's population, in 2014, they suffered only half of one percent of the terrorist deaths, because terrorism is now defined as a phenomenon of war, as part of guerrilla warfare, which happened more in the Middle East and in Asia. Over the long run, terrorist movements sputter out as their small scale violence fails to achieve their strategic goals. We will remember that our terror about terrorism is a sign not of how dangerous our society has become, but how safe.

Peace. For most of human history, war was the national pastime of governments, while peace is just a mere respite between wars. During the feudal times, when warrior kings, ruled by divine right granted to them by the Pope, the chosen representative of God on earth, professional mercenary armies fought according to fixed rules of combat, and the subjects of the king did not really care who won the war, because one king is just about as bad as another, the real owners of the land they till, to whom they must all pay tribute. But when the French Revolution happened in Europe, the divine right of Kings was challenged and Nationalism was born; the people were told that they are no longer the subjects of the King, but free citizens of a republic, bound together by common tongue and a common culture, with a Social Contract with those who govern them, to protect and defend their interest against the interest of other peoples and other nations. No wonder Louis XVI was called the King of <u>France</u>, owner of the land mass, while General Napoleon Bonaparte called himself Emperor of the <u>French</u>, because he chose himself as leader of the people.

The Kings of other countries in Europe woke up to the fact that the principles of the Revolution in Paris had an application far beyond the borders of France, since the doctrine of the sovereignty of the people as the only legitimate foundation of government, challenged the right to exist of every state of Europe ruled by the Divine Right of Kings. At the outset the French Revolution was beset by a deadly struggle for power within, climaxed by Reign of Terror, and a threat of invasion by a coalition of monarchs of countries from without. The threat of invasion aroused in the French a national consciousness, a sense of nationalism that inspired them to repel the invasion and embark on a war of conquest of their own to carry the revolution to the oppressed peoples of Europe. All Europe recognized that a new force has come into the world, and the enemies of France appealed to the nationalism of their own peoples, and not in vain – a reaction to French nationalism when it became a conquering force – realizing that war was no longer a mere ordeal of battle, to be fought out according to fixed rules by professional armies, but a total war with no holds barred, a trial of strength between nations at arms.

Thus the Battle of Leipzig, which practically sealed Napoleon's doom is rightly called the Battle of Nations. Thus sovereignty has ceased to be territorial and became national. Thus, World War I which in 1918 saw the end of the last of the autocratic emperors, the Hapsburg Monarchy, is considered the final and the most stupendous phase (with the use of poison gas, airplanes and tanks) of the Revolution that started with the Fall of Bastille in 1789.

But the sparks of the French Revolution had been carried far and wide and started fires in places unexpected and remote, where they glowed under the surface to burst into flame later. The very first was the Philippine Revolution of 1898 under the 4-year administration of 29-year-old President Emilio Aguinaldo of the First Philippine Republic, until smothered by American Imperialist Forces in 1902. The second was the Chinese Revolution of October 10, 1911, against the Qing Dynasty, the last to rule a 4,000-year ancient civilization that co-existed with ancient Egypt, Greece and Rome – under the Republic of China with 46-year old Sun Yat Sen who ruled as Provisional President for two months from January 1, 1912 to March 5, 1912, until political chaos, multiple governments, civil war, the invasion of Japanese Imperial Forces and World War II intervened.

The total war with no holds barred that is World War II, ended by Unconditional Surrender of Japan with the use of Atomic Bombs on Hiroshima and Nagasaki.

This time the sovereignty of the people and Nationalism that inspired the French Revolution flared up again in the postwar world. The very first again is the Philippines when its independence was restored on July 4, 1945. The second is Indonesia with Declaration of Independence by Sukarno in August 17, 1945, climaxed by the transfer of sovereignty by the Dutch on December 27, 1945. They were followed by India on August 18, 2019 and Malaysia on August 31, 2019. Singapore, Pakistan, Sri Lanka, Myanmar, South and North Korea, Vietnam, Cambodia, Laos, Papua New Guinea, and Algeria along with most nations in Black Africa were liberated upon the utter collapse of Western Colonial Empires.

Rewind a bit back to the year 1945 at the end of World War II. The Cold War is the name given to the relationship that developed primarily between the USA and the USSR after World War II. A clash of very different beliefs and ideology – capitalism versus communism – each held with almost religious conviction, formed the basis of an international power struggle with both sides vying for dominance, exploiting every opportunity for expansion anywhere in the world. The Cold War was to dominate international affairs for decades and many major crises occurred – the Cuban Missile Crisis, Vietnam,

Hungary, and the Berlin Wall, being just some. This was complicated by the involvement of the USA in the Middle East, to secure a reliable source of oil for its economy and war machine and to deny it to others, as well as to guarantee the continued existence of the state of Israel amidst Arab intransigence.

For many, the development of the nuclear fusion hydrogen bomb, several times more powerful than the original nuclear fission Atom Bomb used in World War II, and the subsequent growth of weapons of mass destruction among all major powers on earth and of the intercontinental missiles needed to deliver them to any part of the world, became the most worrisome issue. Yet it is precisely because of this highly probable Mutually Assured Destruction (MAD) that the world powers assiduously avoid crises that may lead to a Hot War that may obliterate mankind. We may have little wars among little nations, or wars among the surrogates of major powers. But World War III among the major powers is no longer an option. We will have peace in our time.

Safety. The human body is a fragile thing, according to Steven Pinker, subject to "the thousand natural shocks that flesh is heir to," easy pickings for predators like crocodiles and lions, and done in by the venom of snakes, spiders and insects. Trapped in the omnivore's dilemma, he could be poisoned by toxic elements of his expansive diets, including fish, beans, roots, seed and mushrooms. As he ventured up a tree in pursuit of fruit and honey, his body obeyed Newton's law of universal gravitation, and was liable to fall and accelerate toward the ground at the rate of 9.8 meters per second per second, and hit the dirt at a force equal to the mass of his body multiplied by the acceleration rate, $F=ma$. If he waded too far into lakes and rivers, he can be sure he would be buoyed up by a force equal to the weight of the water he displaced, according to the Archimedes Principle, but that may not be enough to make him float, so he'd better swim or be drowned. If he played with fire, he sometimes got burned. If his rival in love went after him with malice aforethought, he'd better employ in self defense the same technology with which he could kill an animal for food.

Today, now on top of the food chain, human beings are no longer eaten by predators, but they are still involved in accidents. The most serious of these are vehicular accidents, which consists of 26 percent of all accidents in the USA in 2014. By the way, the Brooklyn

Dodgers were so named, because of the skill they developed dodging trams and cars. Pedestrians' lives are now protected by traffic lights, crosswalks, overpasses and the demise of hood ornaments and other chrome-plated weaponry. Drivers' lives are protected by innovations by the car industry itself: buzzing and garroting seatbelts, padded dash and visors, air bags, and recessed or collapsing steering wheel hub designed not to skewer the driver like kebab during a collision; crumple zones, 4-wheeled brakes, stability control systems. And from the authorities, we get roads paved into lanes, reflectored, guard-railed, smooth-curved, and broad-shouldered highways, and stricter laws on drunk driving. Vehicular accidents declined steadily from 30 per 10,000 in 1937 to 10.2 per 10,000 in 2014; and may go down to zero in the future if we adopt Google's or Tesla's driverless cars, along with Waze algorithms to drive General Motors and Toyota to bankruptcy and rid the world of careless and imperfect human drivers.

Also we suffer from homicides which certainly are not accidents. The horrific mass homicides in Newtown, Charleston, San Bernardino and Orlando have in some ways come to define the United States. In total there were almost 11,000 gun murders, over 21,000 gun suicides, and over 81,000 nonfatal gun injuries that year. Compared to other rich countries, America's gun violence is on another planet. In 2011 the United States had over 400,000 people gunned down, seven times as many as Canada, over 50 times as many as Germany and almost 60 times as many as the United Kingdom.

So can Americans learn something from other countries on keeping its citizens safe? Japan has some of the strictest gun laws in the world. The basic premise of those laws? If you want to own a gun, good luck; Japan's firearm and swords control law states that no person shall possess a firearm. With few narrow exceptions for hunters, the few applying face an intricately designed bureaucratic obstacle course. If strict gun control laws are enforced, the rate of gun deaths plummet. So despite lots of barbaric video games, gun violence barely exists in Japan.

Despite the Swiss people's enthusiasm for guns, gun homicide rates are 15 times lower than in the United States in 2013. Everyone who buys a gun must pass a background check, automatic weapons are banned and gun purchases must be registered with the government. Switzerland may look like a gun utopia, but it combines the availability of firearms with significant gun control. In Australia, mandatory gun registration requires a reason for buying a gun. A ban on semi-automatic rifles and shotguns, and pump-action shotguns eliminated over 600,000 guns, one-fifth of Australia's firearms.

That finally leaves the issue of the American Constitution, the argument of the National Rifle Association (NRA) that the second amendment makes any kind of serious gun control impossible. Warren Burger, chief justice of the Supreme Court for 17 years, a conservative Republican appointed by Richard Nixon, said about the second amendment: "This has been the subject of one of the greatest pieces of <u>fraud</u> -- I repeat the word 'fraud' -- on the American public, by NRA special interest groups, that I have ever seen in my lifetime. Now, just look at those words. There are only three lines to that amendment, and three well-known words 'a well-regulated militia'. If the militia, which was going to be the state army, was going to be well-regulated, why shouldn't 16 and 17 and 18, or any other age persons be regulated in the use of arms?"

One of the most important tasks for a government is to keep its citizens, especially the children, safe on the streets and in their schools. Every other developed country in the world is able to fulfill this basic mandate; America is not. And the greatest tragedy is America knows how to do it, and will not do it.

Democracy. Since 5,000 years ago, the first governments tried to steer a course between the violence of chaos of liberty without restraint, and the violence of wandering bands of armed malefactors preying on the peaceful -- by pacifying the people they ruled, while imposing their own reign of terror that included slavery, human sacrifice, summary executions, and torture and mutilation of dissidents and deviants. Despotism has persisted in history not just because being a despot is nice work if you can get it, but from the people's standpoint, the alternative is even worse. Chaos is deadlier than tyranny.

But between the violence of tyranny and the chaos of liberty without restraint, there is another alternative: Democracy. Democracy may be described as a form of government that threads the needle, exerting just enough force to prevent people from preying on each other, without preying on the people itself. A good democratic government allows people to pursue their lives in safety, protected from the violence of anarchy, and in freedom, protected from the violence of tyranny. For that reason alone, democracy is a major contributor to human flourishing. And that is not the only reason:

democracies, with a few exceptions, also have higher rates of economic growth, fewer wars and genocides, healthier and better-educated citizens, and virtually no famines. If the world has become more democratic over time, that is progress.

In fact, the world has become more democratic, not in a steady rising tide, but in spurts – in three waves. The First Wave was in the 19th century when American constitutional democracy with its checks on government power seemed to be working (despite its continued assault on the blacks and the Indians), followed by the French Revolution with its destruction of the divine right of kings, its Rights of Man, its doctrine of Peoples' Sovereignty and Social Contract between government and governed. This crested to 29 democracies in 1923. This was pushed back by the rise of Fascism, and in 1942, there were only 12 democracies.

The Second Wave began in mid-20th century, when Fascism was defeated, and colonies gained freedom from Western Colonialism, pushing the number of democracies to 36 in 1962. This was pushed back with the rise of Communist totalitarian governments in the Cold War, while the USA retorted by reflection by creating its own horde of tin-horn dictators in Latin America and Southeast Asia. In the 1970s, the prospects for democracy was really bleak.

The Third Wave, no, it was a tsunami, a tidal wave, erupted shortly thereafter. Military and fascist governments fell in Southern Europe – Greece, Spain, Portugal, in the 70s; in Latin America – Argentina, Brazil, Chile in the 80s and 90s; in Asia – Taiwan from Chiang, Philippines from Marcos, South Korea from Chun, Indonesia from Suharto; the Berlin Wall went down in 1989, the Soviet Union collapsed in 1991 and the whole Communist world turned democratic; some African countries overthrew their strong men: and the last European colonies in the Caribbean, opted for independence and democracy.

In 1989, political scientist Francis Fukuyama wrote his famous essay, saying that the rise of liberal democracy signaled "the end of history" -- meaning that the world was coming to a consensus over the most humanly best form of government and no longer has to fight over it.

Equal Rights. For centuries in the past, there was prejudice against minorities of race, religion, gender, age, and sex orientation;

liberation only flowered and flourished in the 21st century and the Third Millennium.

The year 2017 saw the the completion of two terms in office by the first African-American president, Barack Obama, and his wife wrote movingly of the moment she moved into the White House built by black slaves centuries ago. Among the blacks, poverty rate fell from 55% in 1960 to 27.6% in 2011; life expectancy rose from 33 years of age in 1900 (17.6 years below that of the whites) to 75.6 years in 2015 (less than 3 years below that of whites). Black Americans who make it to the age of 65, have longer lives ahead of them than white Americans of the same age. Despite Trump and his white trash base, night raids and lynching of negroes (3 a week at the turn of the 20th century) fell to one, or zero in most years, in the 21st century. In 1950, almost half of the countries in the world had laws that discriminate against ethnic or racial minorities; by 2003, fewer than a fifth did, and they were outnumbered by countries with Affirmative Action policies that favored disadvantaged minorities. Now, that is real progress.

With women's rights, too, the progress is global. In 1900, women can vote only in one country, New Zealand; today they can vote in every country in which men can vote, except one, the Vatican City. Women make up almost 40% of the labor force worldwide, and more than 20% of members of national parliaments. Most countries since 1993 have implemented laws and public awareness campaigns to reduce rape, forced marriage, child marriage, genital mutilation, honor killings, domestic violence, and wartime atrocities. That is also real progress.

Gay rights is another idea whose hour has come. Homosexual acts used to be a criminal offense in almost every country in the world. The first arguments that behavior between consenting adults is nobody's business but their own, were formulated during the Enlightenment by Montesquieu, Voltaire, Baccaria and Bentham. A smattering of countries decriminalized homosexuality soon thereafter, and the number shot up with the gay rights revolution of the 1970s. Though homosexuality is still a crime in more than 70 countries, and a capital crime in 11 Muslim countries, and despite backsliding in Russia and several African nations, there is reason to be optimistic: in 2015, the US Supreme Court legalized gay marriages. Well, that is <u>little</u> progress.

With the rise of life expectancy, and of the votes of the aged, senior citizens and the handicapped are at last rewarded with cash benefits, medical assistance and funeral services, but none as good in the entire world, as in city of Makati, Philippines, where senior citizens like me are entitled as well to birthday cakes, free movies, freedom from color-coded traffic rules and long queue lines in stores, and for Christ's sake, Christmas bonuses! Bless you, Mayor Binay!

The most vulnerable sector of humanity are the children who cannot agitate for their own interests and must depend on the compassion of others. Children all over the world have become better off: they are less likely to enter the world motherless, die before the age of 5, or grow up stunted for lack of food, escaping these assaults of nature, and also human-made ones: they are safer than they were for centuries before, and likelier to enjoy true childhood. In many countries, the law makes grade-school education free and compulsory, making child labor conspicuously illegal, and altogether outlawed. Corporal punishment – the spanking, smacking, paddling, birching, tanning, thrashing – which parents and teachers inflicted on helpless children since the 7th century before Christ, is steadily declining. The only issues unresolved are (1) the US government's (in behalf of the milk industry) and Nestlè's conspiracy to undermine breastfeeding in the face of the UN International Milk Code condemning the malpractices of infant milk marketing, and (2) the Roman Catholic Church's reluctance to stop child molestation by Catholic priests. The worst forms of child exploitation – child prostitution, hazardous labor, child pornography, human trafficking – are condemned internationally, such causes symbolically ratified in 2014 when the Nobel Peace Prize was awarded to Kailash Satyarthi the activist against child labor, and Malala Yousafzai the heroic advocate for girls' education.

Knowledge. And for yet another advance in human progress, we consider the expansion of access to knowledge. Homo Sapiens, the "knowing man", is the species that uses information to resist the rot of entropy and the burdens of evolution. Humans everywhere acquire, accumulate and share knowledge with the use of language, gesture and face-to-face tutelage. At a few times in history, people have hit on technologies that multiply, indeed at an exponential rate, the growth of knowledge, such as writing, printing, and electronic media.

The supernova of knowledge continuously redefines what it means to be human. Our understanding of who we are, where we came from, how the world works and what matters in life, depends on the partaking of the vast and ever-expanding store of knowledge – such awareness truly lifts us to a higher plane of consciousness. It is a gift that belongs to an intelligent species with a long history.

For a long time, knowledge was passed on through story-telling and apprenticeship. Today, it is through schools that it is done. The school which has been a minor social agency, available only to a few, has vastly expanded horizontally and vertically, assuming a significance far in excess of anything the world has ever seen, until it took its place along with the state, the church and the family as one of society's most powerful institutions. Today, education is compulsory in most countries, and is recognized as a fundamental human right by the United Nations.

Could the world be getting not just more literate and knowledgeable, but actually smarter, <u>more intelligent</u>? Amazingly, the answer is YES. Intelligence Quotient (IQ) scores has been rising for more than a century in every part of the world. In schools, in business organizations, in the armed forces, where IQ tests are done wholesale on large numbers of persons, year after year, it has been noticed that IQ scores have been rising at the rate of 3 IQ points every ten years.

I have seen this happen in my own family. At the age of 9 in 1933, when I was in 3rd Grade, Secretary Joseph Hayden of the Department of Public Instruction discovered the IQ test and required himself and all the supervisors, teachers and students in private and public schools to take the test. He showed up later in the hacienda of my grandfather to inform me that I was the smartest in the country with an IQ of 170, which he said is about the same as that of Albert Einstein. Of course I am intelligent, I read one book a day for 70 years and got my degree from the Massachusetts Institute of Technology, the best in the world. But lo and behold, the second generation of my family saw my daughter-in-law, Kim Jacinto Henares, with an IQ of 186, 16 IQ points above mine. And the third generation of my family, my grand-daughter Arianna Henares has an IQ of 190, 20 IQ points above mine! And I don't see the world beating a path to our doors!

When the philosopher James Flynn called attention to this phenomenon (it is now called "The Flynn Effect"), everyone thought it was a mistake or trick, because there certainly was no universal selective breeding of geniuses all over the world, except in Germany under Hitler and it demonstrably did not work. But it is true that we all are getting smarter all over the world: how else can you explain the fact that every grandfather in his 70s has to ask his 10-year-old grandson how to operate the computer?

It really beggars the imagination to think an average person of 1910, if he or she is transported by time machine to the present, would be considered a borderline idiot by today's standards. And conversely, if Mr. or Miss Average of today made the reverse journey back to 1910 by time machine, they would outsmart 98% of the frocked and bewhiskered elite who would greet them as they emerged.

The Game of Thrones. "I am a Man, I am White and Catholic" was the mantra in the time of the Constantine and the Crusades up to the time of the Reformation. "I am a Spaniard too, I alone hold the Ultimate Truth, and am entitled to all the gold of the New World" was the cry at the Age of Discovery and Conquest in the 15th century. "I am an Englishman. I am more white than the Spaniard, God is an Englishman and I am the lord of lands upon which the sun never set!!" was the cry at the time of Shakespeare, Newton and the Industrial Revolution of the 17th century. "I am a Man. I am White, Anglo-Saxon and Protestant," said the waspish American at the dawn of the 20th Century and Manifest Destiny, and added, "I am better than the fucking niggers, the Indians who are better dead, and the Mexicans who are lazy and corrupt. The Spaniards, Italians and Greeks are greasers, the Germans are krauts, the Jews are kikes, the French are frogs, the Russkies are Commies, Filipinos are monkeys with no tails, Arabs are pieces of shit, Asians are coolies, and the English are our cousins, our poor relatives. This is the century of *Pax Americana* and of American Exceptionalism!"

The source of the greatest inequality and conflict, Pinker simply neglected to emphasize, is the pride and prejudice of the tribal instincts of Nations, Religions and Ideologies. Tribes are born to promote the dissensions between Them and Us, to dominate and to rule. They are born and they die too, subject to the rot and decay of Entropy and to the dictates of Evolution, the inevitable defeat at the hands of a stronger rival.

Ancient Egypt got its comeuppance at the Battle of Actium in 31 BC when Octavius defeated the combined forces of Mark Antony and Cleopatra and made Egypt a Roman province. Ancient Rome succumbed to the Catholic Church when Constantine became emperor of the Holy Roman Empire. The Catholic Church lamely limped along after the Protestant Reformation and the French Revolution, till one day I entered the the Church of Notre Dame in Paris one fine Sunday morning, and found it full of foreign tourists, and looked around to see a little side chapel where one Filipino priest officiated mass for about thirty Filipinos…. with my own two eyes, I saw the Church perish, not with a bang, but with a whimper.

It is with immense pride that I find my country the Philippines the actual nemesis of the mighty Spanish Empire. It was here in Mactan when Spain suffered its first defeat, the death of Magellan at the hands of Lapulapu. It was here in the Manila Bay when Spain suffered its final defeat at the hands of Knucklehead George Dewey, one of the most stupid students Annapolis ever produced. And in between, Spain never won a single war. Spain lost its Armada, lost all its colonies in South America to one single man Simon Bolivar, suffered the War of Spanish Succession, was conquered and made a kingdom of Napoleon's brother Joseph, and lost the Philippines, Mexico and the whole American west. And all because Philip II of Spain (after whom the Philippines was named) had all the gold of the Incas, Aztecs and the Mayas, and did not feel the need to industrialize.

The French Revolution destroyed in one fell swoop European Feudalism and the Divine Right of Kings, with the cry of *Libertè, Egalitè, Fraternitè* in the 19th century. The mighty British Empire upon which the sun never set, finally disappeared over the horizon, its wealth and vitality sapped in two World Wars, and in the wake of the ideas and ideals of the French Revolution which liberated all its colonies in the 20th century. At this point the United States of America stood as a colossus as the greatest power on earth, its industrial might untouched by war, its dollar the international currency, its military might and Atom Bomb unchallenged over all lands and seas.

It is in the nature of the strongest kid in the block to push his weight around, and install himself as the A-number One, Head of the List, King of the Hill, Top of the Heap. What was true for Frank Sinatra is true for the United States of America which became the biggest bully on the planet, surrounding its rival the Soviet Union with a string of bases in Canada, Japan, South Korea, Taiwan, Philippines, Pakistan, Middle East, West Germany, Great Britain – while branding the USSR the aggressor and threatening to go to war over a one single

Soviet base in Cuba. The American spy agency CIA was let loose to impose a whole gang of tin-horn dictators in the Middle East (Shah of Iran, Saddam Hussein of Iraq, the monarchy of Saudi Arabia) to secure oil for its industry and war machine; Rafael Trujillo of the Dominican Republic, Papa Doc and Baby Doc Duvalier of Haiti, Anastacio Somosa of Nicaragua, Augusto Pinochet of Chile, the militarists Videla and Galtieri of Argentina, Fulgencio Batista of Cuba, Manuel Noriega of Panama, Chiang Kai-chek of China and Taiwan, Syngman Rhee and Park Chung Hee of South Korea, Ngo Diem of South Vietnam, Lon Nol of Kampuchea, Marcos of the Philippines -- and all the rest of the dictators who kick the teeth of their own people, in the interest of Uncle Sam, carpetbaggers of the United Fruit variety, and advocates of the Low Intensity Conflict policy to save American lives at the expense of other peoples. The US policy was to make the Philippines the vegetable garden to supply food and raw materials to its fast developing allies Taiwan, South Korea and Japan; and to do so, the CIA and US-AID sabotaged our Land Reform Program; and President Lyndon Johnson himself told our leaders with his customary frank and threatening manner to stop industrialization and concentrate on "export-oriented labor-intensive agricultural program of development." I ought to know, I was then Chairman of the National Economic Council of the Republic of the Philippines.

All these above, Pinker neglects to mention, and often blames the "tribal" Nationalism of nations as an obstacle to worldwide unity under the aegis of the United Nations and the New Enlightenment. I do not agree, Nationalism is what motivates poor nations to liberate and assert themselves and achieve political, economic and cultural development. It leads to the idea of unity amid diversity. It is the EXCESS of Nationalism of powerful nations that negates Nationalism of others and constitutes Imperialism, a divisive force that causes colonial exploitation by the strategy of Divide and Conquer. The notion of American Exceptionalism is corollary to American Manifest Destiny, American Imperialism, and Donald Trumps' America First Policy. The totalitarian Soviet bloc of nations, no angels either, collapsed by 1991.

In the 21st century of the Third Millennium, time has come for the comeuppance of international bullies, strengthen the United Nations and the Globalism of which Trump says, "America is governed by Americans. We reject the ideology of globalism, and we embrace the doctrine of patriotism. Around the world, responsible nations must defend against threats to sovereignty not just from global governance, but also from other, new forms of coercion and domination." How to accomplish this is not the subject of this book, but of the one I have already written, *The Rise of China: Games that Nations Play*, published by Amazon.com.

Chapter 14.
The Destiny of Man

Part 1. Virgin births in the future!

What is the future of Man? Man has progressed more in the last fifty years than in the first five million years of his existence. Man has within living memory learned to split and fuse the atom, and acquire a source of power equal to those of suns and stars. Man now knows how to free himself from Mother Earth, and reach out into the timeless space beyond.

More exciting than Nuclear Power and the Race to the Stars, is the coming Biological Revolution. Man can shape his world, yes, but he is also learning how to shape himself.

We already have artificial insemination that makes it possible for a woman to bear the child of a man she has never met. Now it is possible for a woman to bear another woman's child.

Dr. E.S.F. Hafez at Washington State University pioneered in techniques that make it possible, a few years hence, for a housewife to walk into a store, look down a row of packages not unlike flower-seed packages, and pick her baby by the label.

Each packet would contain a frozen embryo one-day-old, and the label would tell the shopper what color of hair and eyes to expect as well as the probable size and IQ of the child. It would also offer assurance of freedom from genetic defects.

After making her selection, the lady could take the packet to her doctor and have the embryo implanted in herself, where it would grow for nine months, like any baby of her own. A virgin birth, no less. Husbands and lovers no longer necessary.

Dr. Daniele Petrucci of Bologna, Italy, was able to conceive and grow a human embryo outside of the womb, until he was forced to terminate his experiments, by an irate citizenry condemning his manipulating human life in this fashion.

Other scientists, including the Russians and at least two Americans -- Dr. John Rock at Harvard and Dr. Landum B. Shettles at Columbia-Presbyterian Hospital in New York -- had grown embryos in vitro (in glass) along the same line of research.

More advanced vitro culture techniques are in the offing. Already it is commonplace to keep alive various kinds of human cells in tissue culture for long periods of time, growing whole colonies from single cells again and again. It has been seriously suggested that it may be possible eventually to grow an entire organ like a kidney or a liver in tissue culture.

Some years ago, the eminent French biologist Jean Rostand even predicted that a man might someday be able to have a culture of his own cells stashed away somewhere so that a complete replica of himself could be grown in case he met with an untimely accident.

Impossible? Dr. Frederick C. Steward of Cornell University had achieved exactly this sort of sexual reproduction with a lowly carrot. As a result, Dr. Rostand predicted that tissue culture techniques "would in theory enable us to create as many identical individuals as might be desired. A living creature would be printed in hundreds, in thousands of copies, all of them real twins. This would in short be human propagation by cuttings, by xeroxing, assuring the indefinite reproduction of the same individual -- of a great man, for example."

Would anyone like to name the great man he would care to see duplicated by the dozen, by the hundreds, by the thousands? Just think of having 30 million Ferdinand Marcoses to make this nation great again!

Of all the variations that may be played upon the theme of human procreation, the ultimate will be the production of human beings whose specifications can be drawn in advance. This could come about through the manipulation of the genetic material itself -- deoxyribonucleic acid or DNA.

When that time comes, Man's powers will be truly godlike. He may bring into being creatures never before seen or imagined in the universe. He may even choose to create new forms of humanity -- a being that may be better adapted to survive in the airless surface of the moon, or on the bottom of the Pacific Ocean.

Even without going that far, Man presumably will be able to write out any set of specifications he might desire for his ideal human being. This is what scientists mean when they talk of Man controlling his own evolution, when they say we are in a biological revolution that will more than any other scientific advances -- even more than nuclear power or the race to the stars -- determine the final destiny of Man.

Part 2. DNA and the Future of Man

THE future of Man depends on his knowledge and use of the genetic material called deoxyribonucleic acid or DNA. In the coiled structure of the DNA molecule and the complex arrangements of its atoms lie the final secrets of life and heredity. The DNA is present in all life -- in a microbe, a tree, a fish or a human being -- the immortal carrier of life on earth. For all its potency and complexity, the DNA molecule is infinitesimally tiny, yet in one single cell is crammed instructions that would fill several 24-volume sets of Encyclopedia Britannica. Instructions in the DNA are written out in a four-letter code, each "letter" being a specific chemical substance.

Just as 26 letters of our Roman alphabet can spell out millions of stories, poems, novels and textbooks; just as 10 digits of Arabic numerals can spell out millions of formulas, scientific laws and solutions thereof; just as the two digits of the computers can work out the most complicated calculations of a thousand lifetimes in a split second of time -- the four-letter code of the DNA molecule gives out instructions that will make of a single cell any of the millions of earth's creatures: an elephant, a worm, a germ, a vegetable or a human being. Scientists are beginning to "read" this genetic code -- but only in a halting incipient way, and it may take a long time before they become really fluent readers. But once they can read, they may begin to "write" -- that is to give genetic instructions in the genetic code. Several bio-engineering patents have already been given to scientists who invented new kinds of microbes to produce drug cures and instruments of biological warfare.

In time scientists may be able to create new forms of humanity -- one that can survive the trip to planets a million light-years away, or another to work under tremendous water pressure on the ocean bottom. Or they may be able to create an ideal man with a desirable set of specifications.

Man can sure stand some improvement, but who shall we appoint to play God for us? Which scientist, statesmen, artist, judge, poet, philosopher, educator -- of which nation, race or creed -- will we trust to write the specifications, to decide which characteristics are most ideal?

This is the supreme challenge to Man today: the "Grand Option" which urgently confronts not only our leaders, but each and every single one of us. A decision to let things ride or ignore this biological revolution is simply a decision to turn it over to any unscrupulous opportunist who chooses to employ it for his own ends.

We need only to imagine some totalitarian nation of the future, led by a man who is sure he knows what is best for everybody. He has at his command all the new means of controlling reproduction, the human brain and behavior.

He can raise entire populations in vitro or tissue culture, on a set of specifications he alone will decide -- a mass of workers here, an army of fighters there, drones, queen bees -- like an efficient beehive -- maintaining his subjects in a constant state of euphoria by stimulating the pleasure centers of the brain. Practically no one in such a society would have any true choice, but everybody would be "happy." If everybody is happy, can anything be wrong?

If we think so, says Sir Julian Huxley, we must ascertain once again that we know the answer to the basic question: What are people for? What is the purpose of human existence?

Without an answer to such questions we remain helpless to use scientific advance as it should be used -- as a tool to serve human values in a democratic society.

We can make things happen beyond our wildest dreams. But what ought to happen? There are powerful institutions to give us guidance about what ought to happen -- the most powerful being religion. Regardless of what science makes possible, moral approval or disapproval has, throughout man's history, influenced which advances he accepts instantly, which he accepts more slowly and which he rejects altogether. In the new age however, it is unlikely that any scientific advance can be totally ignored even by religion.

Scientists themselves are trying hard to build their own codes and standards out of logic and scientific knowledge. The growing movement is called Scientific Humanism. Influential on it have been such figures as Sir Julian Huxley, author of Religion Without Revelation and the late French Jesuit priest-scientist-philosopher Pierre Teillard de Chardin (tilard de zhardan) who wrote *The Future of Man* and *The Phenomenon of Man*.

Part 3. Grand Option: eternal life as part of God.
ONE man flying in the face of appearance, perceived that the forces of nature depicts the flow of a tremendous tide, and cried out to Mankind peacefully slumbering on the raft of Earth, "We are moving forward!"

Part of mankind, startled by the look-out's cry, has left the huddle where the rest of the crew slumbered. Gazing over the dark sea, they study for themselves the lapping of waters along the hull of the craft that bears them, breathe the scents borne to them on the breeze, gaze at the shadows cast from pole to pole by a changeless eternity.

And all things while remaining separately the same -- the ripple of the water, the scent of the air, the lights in the sky -- become linked together and acquire a new sense: the fixed and random Universe is seen to move.

No one who has seen this vision can be restrained from guarding and proclaiming it!

Thus began The Future of Man by Pierre Teilhard de Chardin (tilard de zhardan), a French Jesuit priest-scientist-philosopher who along with Sir Julian Huxley is trying to unravel the mysteries of the final destiny of Man.

Father de Chardin extrapolated the past into the future, and had to invent new words to describe the future of man -- homonisation, complexification, christogenesis. He saw Man as the only creature that interbreeds -- black, white, yellow, brown races all interbreeding, while other creatures evolved into widely separated species. Birds have 8,500 separate species, the insects over half a million.

Man is converging or enfolding upon himself. Not only is he interbreeding, but he is interthinking. Through contact with one another, the speeding of the means of communication, and ever denser tangle of economic and social relationships, mankind has found itself seized in the mold of a communal existence -- a biological and mental compression that will precede the death of humanity as we know it now, and our rebirth in another evolutionary stage -- which he called Ultra-Humanism.

"Pressed tightly against one another by the increase of their numbers and relationships, forced together by the growth of common power and a sense of common travail, the men of the future will in some way form a single consciousness" -- like the different cells of the body, separate but interrelated and united in thought and deed, as if we were all part of one universal body and mind.

Does de Chardin mean that the man of the future will submerge his individuality to a super organization -- like ants or bees? He himself says that all this "Total Homonisation" will come to us voluntarily, of our own free will in the exercise of our "Grand Option." De Chardin writes in mystic terms hard to understand. Man must destroy and recreate himself. But what will ultra humanity be like? Chardin himself does not know, but let me hazard a guess.

Suppose I was empowered to recreate the human being, to write out the specifications in DNA code for the next stage of human evolution. I will create human brains capable of mental and sensual telepathy, so that each man can think and feel through the brains of another, so that each of us can absorb the knowledge and skills of the greatest scientist, the greatest doctor, engineer, poet, philosopher, and participate in the adventure of a man climbing the highest peak, in the delights of another making love to a beautiful woman, or another listening to great music, or another feasting his sights on a beautiful painting. There will be no selfishness because in mind and senses we are all united. There will be no ignorance, poverty or injustice -- for what is experienced by one will be experienced by all. Our bodies may die, but each will renew existence in the mind and body of another - like brain cells that die and are replaced in a continuously living brain. We shall all indeed be part of one universal eternal consciousness, one Being that we cannot do better than simply call God -- for did not Christ promise that we shall all someday be united in one Mystical Body?

Teilhard de Chardin ends his book The Future of Man with these beautiful words:

Like a vast tide the Being will have dominated the trembling of all beings. The extraordinary adventure of the World will have ended in the bosom of a tranquil ocean, of which however, each drop will still be conscious of being itself. The dream of every mystic will have found its full and proper fulfillment. Erit in omnibus omnia Deus.

In a world racing madly towards nuclear self-destruction, we are offered a Grand Option: eternal life as part of God.

Chapter 15.
Lead and the Age of the Earth

The scientist who discovered the age of the Earth also helped end the use of lead in gasoline and other products in the United States.

One episode of National Geographic "Cosmos: A Spacetime Odyssey" explored the life of Clair Patterson, a geochemist who pinpointed Earth's age for the first time and also uncovered a secret: Lead contamination is a major and potentially deadly problem. The newest episode of "Cosmos," called "The Clean Room," takes viewers on a tour of Patterson's work and the industry that fought him as he tried to learn more about lead and its harmful effects.

Patterson's work initially focused on the Earth's age. Many scientists had tried to date the age of the planet before Patterson, using sedimentary layers in geology work, especially that of the layers of the Grand Canyon to measure the Earth's age based on layers of material laid down over long spans of time.

"We know from observing this process, because it still happens today in oceans and lakes around the world, that sediments can be laid down at widely different rates," the host Neil Tyson said. "It usually happens very slowly, say a foot of sediment per 1,000 years, but when there's a rare catastrophic flood, it can happen much faster, as much as a foot in a just a few days."

Before Patterson conducted his work, scientists had tried to use the layers of sediment to estimate the age of the Earth. Because the sediment was laid down at different rates, however, the researchers' numbers were wildly different and the findings didn't stand the test of time.

Patterson came up with different numbers, using a method different in his experiments. He was enlisted to measure the amount of lead in zircon crystals from a fragment of a meteorite — a leftover space rock from the dawn of the solar system — to better understand the age of the Earth. Eventually, Patterson moved to the California Institute of Technology, where he created the first scientific clean room to try to get a proper reading on his crystals.

For 6 long years, Patterson doggedly tracked down and eliminated the many sources of lead that were compromising his instruments, said 'Cosmos' host Neil deGrasse Tyson during the show: "He had built the world's first ultra-clean room. He was finally able to measure how much lead was actually in the rock, one whose age had already been established. Now, at last, Patterson was ready to tackle the iron meteorite."

Eventually, after years of research, Patterson was able to say that the Earth was born about 4.5 billion years ago, to be exact, an age of 4.55 ± 0.07 billion years, very close to today's accepted age, which was determined by Clair Cameron Patterson using uranium-lead isotope dating (specifically lead-lead dating) on several meteorites including the Canyon Diablo meteorite and published in 1956.

But before arriving at that final answer, the scientist had to overcome some difficulties. As Patterson tried to measure the lead in his zircon crystals, he kept getting wildly different results. Slowly but surely, Patterson realized that lead was contaminating many things in the environment.

He learned that using lead in gasoline meant spewing the contaminant into the environment, potentially poisoning children and adults. Eventually this led to Lead ban in the U.S.A.

When in ancient Rome, don't drink as the Romans do. High-born Romans sipped beverages cooked in lead vessels and channeled spring water into their homes through lead pipes. Some historians argue that lead poisoning plagued the Roman elite with diseases such as gout and hastened the empire's fall.

The levels of lead Patterson found in the environment were not natural, as petroleum industry officials claimed. Instead, human-made products containing lead affected the environment and public health, Tyson said. For humans, even trace amounts of lead are unsafe, Tyson said during the show. After much time and effort, Patterson's scientific work with lead paid off, leading to a ban on lead in products like gasoline, canned goods and paint in the United States.

Chapter 16.
The Cosmic Year Tabulated

"Cosmic Year" is a way to conceptualize the age of the universe (13.8 billion years). At this scale, there are 437.5 years per second, 26.250 thousand years per minute, 1.575 million years per hour, 37.8 million years per day, 1.2 billion years per month, and Homo Sapiens evolved only 14 minutes before midnight in the last hour of the Cosmic Year.

If the age of the universe were compressed into one year…

DATE/TIME: **EVENT**

January 1, 12:00:01 AM: In the first second of the Cosmic Year, on New Year's Eve, the Big Bang happened and the universe is born, 13.8 billion years ago, from a single atom so dense that it contained all the elements of our universe. We can only speculate, and we will never really know, what the universe was like before the Big Bang. Nothing but Darkness for the next 2 billion years.

January 14   Then Light in the form of a gamma ray burst, appeared.

January 22   The first small galaxy appeared.

March 15   Our galaxy, the Milky Way, was born of stardust.

May 12   The Milky Way disc, as we see it now, was formed.

September 2   The Solar System was formed.

September 6   Our own earth was born 4.5 billion years ago, followed by the moon.

September 14   3.5 billion years ago, life originated under the oceans, made out of single-celled creatures, eating each other.

November 9   One single cell could not ingest the other single cell it had just eaten.

December 5   The multi-celled creature came into being.

December 7   Sex was born and saw an explosion of life on earth, finally dominated by the dinosaurs.

December 20   The first plant and flower appeared.

December 30   An asteroid was deflected in its path and collided with the earth, landing in Arizona. The death of dinosaurs happened shortly thereafter, 13.5 million years ago. The earth tilted

23 degrees from its axis, and the seasons were born in the northern and southern hemispheres.

December 31, 8:03 PM   3 hours and 57 minutes before the end of the cosmos year, 6 million years ago, a single female ape gave birth to two daughters, one of whom became the ancestor of chimpanzees, the other the ancestor of Homo Sapiens, and his cousins Homo Erectus, Neanderthal, Homo Soloensis, Homo Floresienses, Homo Donisova.

December 31, 10:41 PM   1 hour and 19 minutes before the end of the cosmos year, 2 million years ago Homo Erectus, our cousin, evolved and died out 73,000 years before we of the Homo Sapiens even existed.

December 31, 11:46 PM   14 minutes before midnight on the last day of the Cosmic Year, 70,000 years ago, Homo Sapiens evolved, as hunters and gatherers, with Cognitive powers that allowed him to cooperate, even with strangers, which no other earthly species could replicate.

December 31, 11:55 PM   5 minutes before midnight, 60,000 years ago, Homo was able to domesticate Fire for light, protection and cooking food.

December 31, 11:58 PM   2 minutes before midnight, in the last hour of the last day of the Cosmic Year, 55,000 years ago, Man painted his first picture.

December 31, 11:58:07 PM 1 minute and 53 seconds before midnight, 50,000 years ago, our cousins, Homo Soloensis and Homo Donisova, ceased to exist.

December 31, 11:58:51 PM 1 minute and 9 seconds before midnight, 30,000 years ago, our cousins, the Neanderthals, ceased to exist.

December 31, 11:58:58 PM 1 minute and 2 seconds before midnight, 12,000 years ago, the last of our close cousins, the dwarf-like Homo Floresiensis, ceased to exist. It seems that every time Homo Sapiens moved into any location, the local population of plants and large animals simply died out, leaving Homo Sapiens the ONLY human species alive, and the master of planet earth.

December 31, 11:59:32 PM 28 seconds before midnight, 10,000 years ago agriculture was invented, followed by an irreversible population explosion, and the human race began to settle in towns and cities.

December 31, 11:59:33 PM The next second was the end of the Ice

Age.

December 31, 11:59:48 PM 12 seconds to midnight, the Egyptian and Chinese Civilization came into being.

December 31, 11:59:49 PM 11 seconds to midnight the first writing appeared and the wheel was invented.

December 31, 11:59:54 PM 6 seconds to midnight, Buddha, Confucius, Euclid and Archimedes and the Ancient Greek Civilization were born.

December 31, 11:59:55 PM 5 seconds to midnight, Jesus Christ and the Roman Empire were born, and the number zero was invented.

December 31, 11:59:56 PM 4 seconds to midnight, Mohammad, the Maya Civilization and the Byzantine Empire came into being.

December 31, 11:59:58 PM 2 seconds to midnight, the Mongol Empire, the Crusades, Christopher Columbus and the Age of Discovery, the Renaissance, Johann Sebastian Bach and Shakespeare happened.

December 31, 11:59:59 PM On the last second of the cosmic year, Isaac Newton and the Scientific Revolution were born, only 500 years ago, along with Capitalism, Industrialization, and the three of the most staggering developments of all time: (1) exploiting the power of suns and stars, (2) reaching out to the timeless space beyond our planet, (3) probing the secrets of the DNA, and controlling our own evolution. The USA, World War I, World War II, Albert Einstein, Karl Marx, Adolf Hitler, and President Franklin Delano Roosevelt came into being.

December 31, 12:00:00 PM On the last tick of the last second of the cosmic year, man landed on the moon, and a new chapter in history of the human race begins. With his power to manipulate the DNA, Homo Sapiens can now control his own evolution to the next level, Homo Deus, perhaps?

About the Author:

Dr. Hilarion M. Henares, Jr., Doctor of Economics, will probably be known as the Alexander Hamilton of the Philippines. As Hamilton argued for his "Theory of Manufactures" to point the way to the United States' emergence as an industrial power, against Thomas Jefferson's advocacy of a "pastoral economy", so did Henares argue for Philippine Industrialization against American policy to keep the Philippines agricultural.

More than anyone else Henares is the most eloquent spokesman for the Philippine industrial middle class, and he articulated for his generation, the Nationalist Economic Philosophy for the advancement of the common masses. Said Education Secretary Juan Manuel, "Fiercely nationalistic, Henares chose as his field of battle the area of economics. There are many milestones that mark our way to economic emancipation and Henares was there first. He was a visionary, a gadfly, an achiever... who prodded this country almost against its will to accept the challenge of change in the postwar years."

Henares studied in the best schools, Ateneo de Manila, University of the Philippines and the Massachusetts Institute of Technology, but his early schooling was in the public schools, where his Senator grandfather put him to prepare him for a political career; he became a cabinet member and a senatorial candidate together with Ninoy Aquino in 1967. At the age of 30, he was already the head of a multi-million peso business enterprise. Henares became the President of the powerful Philippine Chamber of Industries, and eventually a member of the presidential cabinet as the Chairman of the National Economic Council and Presidential Administrator on Community Development. "One of the most brilliant of my cabinet," said President Diosdado Macapagal, the fifth President of the Philippine Republic. Henares was at the age of 25, the dean of two graduate schools. He made one movie and it won the FAMAS Academy Award as the Best Documentary of the Year 1957. He sired six children, and was awarded the Presidential Award for Exemplary Family Life by Malacañang Palace in 1960. He was Young Businessman of the Year 1959 and Industrialist of the Year 1963.

He was a newspaper columnist (front page column "Ways and Means" in pre-martial law Manila Times and in post-Edsa's "Make My Day!" in the Philippine Daily Inquirer, and in the Manila

Standard), an essayist, a poet, a TV and radio commentator and a public speaker much in demand. He is now on UNTV owned by his son (UHF 37, Cable 58) at primetime 7:45 PM 5 days a week, Monday through Friday; simulcast on radio DWUN-am (1350 KHz), Monday through Friday. His website is www.philippinefolio.com.

He was the Presidential Consultant on National Affairs, to President Gloria Macapagal Arroyo whose father he served, and to President Fidel V. Ramos, a friend of his youth, who assigned him confidential tasks of national import, and took him along on State Visits. He was an Eisenhower Fellow in the USA, an official guest and negotiator of treaties in Great Britain, Israel, Germany, the People's Republic of China, Indonesia, Soviet Union, and an official representative to conferences abroad. He is a radio amateur, a computer buff, an electronic expert who makes his own television sets, quadrophonic equipment, electronic organ, and burglar alarms; a photography and movie enthusiast; a gun and book collector. Above all, he is a Nationalist in the great tradition of Claro M. Recto and Jose Rizal, an indefatigable champion of the nationalist cause, whose speeches and writings will show the way and the light for future generations of Filipinos. He is at the end of 2018, an old man of 94 years of ago, still in full possession of his faculties.

END OF THE BOOK

Appendix X

HENARES BOOKS AVAILABLE WORLDWIDE

<u>MAKE MY DAY SERIES</u>

BK 1: MAKE MY DAY	BK 2: NICE AND NASTY
BK 3: CECILIA, MY LOVE	BK 4: SWEET AND SOUR
BK 5: SAINTS AND SINNERS	BK 6: VILLAINS AND HEROES
BK 7: TOUGH AND TENDER	BK 8: LIGHT AND SHADOW
BK 9: GIVE AND TAKE	BK 10: TO BE OR NOT TO BE
BK 11: CASH AND CREDITS	BK 12: RISE AND FALL
BK 13: SWANS AND SWINE	BK 14: TOUCH AND GO
BK 15: LIFE AND DEATH	BK 16: KISS AND BITE
BK 17: GOOD AND EVIL	BK 18: BEAST AND BEAUTY
BK 19: BEGGAR AND KING	BK 20: TRASH AND TREASURES
BK 21: WEAR AND TEAR	BK 22: ANGEL AND DEVIL
BK 23: PRETTY UGLY	BK 24: SALVATION & DAMNATION
BK 25: HEAVEN AND HELL	BK 26: RAGS AND RICHES
BK 27: JOY AND SORROW	BK 28: CALM AND STORMY
BK 29: CLEAN AND DIRTY	BK 30: LEAD AND GOLD
BK 31: BAD AND GOOD	BK 32: THEN NOW THENCE
BK 33: HOT AND COLD	BK 34: LESS AND MORE
BK 35: STOP AND GO	BK 36: LOVE AND HATE
BK 37: ZERO AND INFINITY	BK 38: FIRST AND LAST
BK 39: VICTORY AND DEFEAT	BK 40: ALPHA AND OMEGA

BIOGRAPHICAL SERIES:

<u>The Moving Finger Writes</u>: Love Letters, Cecilia and Larry Henares; <u>Hilarion G. Henares, Life and Times</u>: by Edith Perez de Tagle & Hilarion M. Henares Jr.; <u>Daniel Maramba, Life and Times</u>: by Edith Perez de Tagle & Hilarion M. Henares Jr.; <u>THE LARRY</u>, by Elvira L. Henares-Esguerra

ANTHEM SERIES:

<u>With Fervor Burning</u>; <u>Behold the Radiance</u>; <u>Suns and Stars Alight</u>; <u>For Us Thy Sons</u>

LEGACY SERIES:

<u>Dawn of Great Civilizations</u>, heralding the return of the Mother Principle; <u>The Milk Wars,</u> Casualties of Corporate Greed; <u>Economics</u> for those who flunked the course; <u>Philippine History and the Destiny of the Filipino People</u>; <u>These Made Me Smile</u>; <u>Memories of the Great and the Famous</u>; <u>In Search of Perfection</u>; <u>Magnum Opus Dei</u>; <u>Opus Dei and the CIA</u>; <u>Opus Dei, Pirates and Parasites</u>; <u>Ipis Dei, Cockroach of God</u>; <u>Rise of China</u>, Games that Nations Play; <u>Footlights and Shadows</u>; <u>Of Time and Space, Of God and Man</u>; THE SINATRA SONG BOOK.